3

259,-

GW01464133

BLAŽEJ KOVÁČ

THE WEST
TATRAS

COMPILED BY: DANIEL KOLLÁR

The West Tatras (Západné Tatry)
1st edition, 2001

Editors: Peter Augustini and Daniel Kollár
Hiking tours: Blažej Kováč
Natural settings: Ján Lacika
Natural landmarks and points of interests: Daniel Kollár
Responsible editor: Daniel Kollár
Technical editor: Tibor Kollár
Translation: HACON
Photographs: Karol Demuth, Ladislav Janiga, Miroslav Vážny
Attitude profiles: Ján Lacika
Cartography: © Vojenský kartografický ústav, š. p., Harmanec, 2001
Cover: Ján Hladík
Design and layout: Jagus DTP
Print: Kníhtlačiareň Svornosť, a.s., Bratislava

This guidebook is also available in the Slovak, English, German and Polish languages. Any, including partial, use of this work is permitted only with the written consent of GEOINFO Slovakia Foundation and DAJAMA publications. The publisher is not liable to legal responsibility for the way of use of this guidebook.

© GEOINFO Slovakia, Ľubľanská 2,831 02 Bratislava
© DAJAMA, Klimkovičova 1, 841 01 Bratislava
ISBN 80–88975–24–7

Dear readers,

The purpose of the ĽAJAMA publishers since the beginning of its existence is to promote the regions of Slovakia publishing guidebooks to its geographical and historical assets. Within the series **Regions without frontiers** the individual boundary areas were presented and the series Visiting Slovakia introduced the potential reader to the history and present of the natural historic regions. All books are prepared not only in the Slovak language but also in several foreign languages. Precisely the translations of our guidebooks represent the principal aim of our activities based in the idea to make the attractiveness of Slovakia accessible also to tourists coming from abroad.

The new series **Knapsacked Travel in Slovakia** has been prepared with similar intention. Four books will be published in this series in 2001: The West Tatras (Západné Tatry), The Low Tatras (Nízke Tatry), The Slovak Paradise (Slovenský raj), and The High Tatras (Vysoké Tatry) in four languages: Slovak, English, German, and Polish. As the title of the series suggests, the guidebooks are intended for hikers above all. They contain descriptions of tours, maps illustrating the routes, altitude profiles, classification by exactness and time schedules complemented by photographs of the typical sceneries in most cases. Introduction to the individual books also contains general information, basic characteristics of natural setting of the area in question, and a map of the region with indicated situation of the individual tours. The guidebook also highlights natural landmarks and special points of interests, options to trips, practical information and a register of the most important hiking points.

All recommended tours were written leaning on personal experience of the authors and collaborators. In spite of it, minor changes and discrepancies are possible. We apologize for them and will be grateful if you let us know of any such discrepancy that you may detect. We shall use the information in future editions.

Dear readers,

We are sincerely convinced that you will choose the ideal trip for you from our offer of routes in the most beautiful mountain ranges of Slovakia and will have good time in the romantic setting of the Slovak mountains. We wish you good weather, high spirit and, of course, happy home-coming.

Peter Augustini and Daniel Kollár

Contents

How to use the guidebook

The series Knapsacked Travel in Slovakia is intended for hikers. The introductory part of the book is dedicated to general information on how to plan the individual trips and the basic principles of movement in nature. The first chapter briefly characterizes the natural conditions (starting with surface forms over the waters, climate, soils, vegetation and wild life, ending by the conservation aspect) of the territory in question. A map of the region in scale 1:500 000, which contains the numbered described hiking routes follows.

Then comes the detailed description of the individual routes. A list of the most important information arranged in entries opens each route description. The first entry is the situation of the territory of the route. The second entry is the starting point with the name of the place where the trip starts and the way how to get there (bus stop of SAD = Slovak Bus Transports or the station of ŽSR which means the Railways of the Slovak Republic, a parking lot). The third entry is the finishing point of the route, the place, where the trip ends and the way now to get from there (again bus stop, railway station or parking lot). The fourth entry contains the schedule and the list of the points of the route accompanied by the time that an average hiker needs get to the next point (the time used for relaxing or sightseeing is not included). The fifth entry is information on altitude difference, i.e. the difference between the lowest and the highest points of the trip. The last entry recommends the map of territory of interest, the hiker should have at hand. They are normally available in the local bookstores or newspaper stalls.

Classification of the tour as to degree of difficulty and description of the basic tour follows. The description emphasizes the landmarks. Part of each route is the cutting of map with outlined course of the tour. Medium

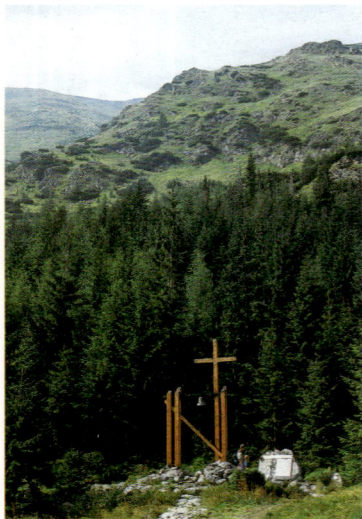

Piety place

demanding and demanding routes are also characterised by the altitude profile while the information is complemented by a photograph illustrating the typical setting. Basic routes are compiled in a way, which includes all important areas of the territory. However, the routes are in no way definite. They are rather recommendations, which can be modified or combined (if you overnight in a mountain hotel, for instance) or shortened. Some trips also contain options.

Classification of trips

The proposed routes run normally on well-marked hiking paths and roads. The hiker is always warned of possible orientation trouble. It means increased attention and frequent use of map. All kinds of hikers — from the experienced and fit ones to the inexperienced and comfort-preferring ones — can choose from our offer. The colour of the route numbers, green, blue or red, express three degrees of the trips: little demanding, moderately demanding and demanding routes.

Easy routes are marked in green and they are suitable for older people, families with children and less fit tourists. They are mostly half-day outings running on good roads or paths with low altitude difference and rather short. Medium demanding tours are marked in blue. They are intended for fit hikers and families with grown-up children. They are longer and the altitude difference is higher. Some of them also require orientation sense and some experience with movement in nature. The red-marked tours are for the above-average hikers in excellent physical condition who are used to all-day walk, high altitude difference, use of climbing aids and difficult orientation, and who possess sufficient experience in movement in difficult terrain.

Outfit

The tours in mountain and high-mountain environment always require an adequate outfit and equipment, suitable clothes and footwear including. Plimsolls or low shoes do not protect against injuries in rocky terrain, especially not on moving debris. Also suitable underwear (special thermo-underwear) is important and the upper Polar garments of different thickness are ideal for unstable weather only too frequent in mountains. Weather-proof jackets and trousers (preferably Goratex made) as the top outfit is recommended as well. You will certainly need a plastic mack, cap, mittens, thermo-isolating foil for emergency situations, and the basic medical kit on long and demanding tours. Ski poles and climbing irons even hatchet are recommended if there are snow fields on the route. You should also carry your ID, a watch, map and guidebook, sufficient food and drinks and a disposal bag (to carry the offal back, do not leave it there). Warm clothes are recommended even in hot summer months as the sudden change of weather can be very unpleasant for a hiker lacking the adequate outfit.

Ten basic principles for safe stay in the mountains

1. Chose the tour fitting your possibilities.
2. Inquire about the chosen tour and its state at the nearest Mountain Rescue Service station.
3. Let your host (person in charge of the establishment where you are accommodated) know about the aim of the tour and expected time of return, and write it in the book of trips before you leave.
4. If you are going away for a longer trip always start in the morning.
5. Your footwear should be solid even in sunny weather.
6. Always have waterproof garments at hand.
7. You should go back if the weather starts to deteriorate.
8. Always stick to the marked trail, do not venture into unknown parts and do not step on snow fields.
9. If the trail above the upper timber line is covered by snow and there are not marking poles in sight, it is considered not marked and you must not continue on it.
10. If you cannot return to the place where you are accommodated, you should notify your host.

Ten basic principles of safe hiking

1. Study the map of your the trip and read the guidebook in advance.
2. Always concentrate on the key points of the routes, especially the crossroads.
3. Abrupt changes of direction or turnings onto less important communications are indicated by a sign (arrow).
4. If you do not find marking in the course of say 300 m where there are enough objects suitable for placing a mark, you have probably gone astray. In that case it is better to go back to the nearest crossroads and find the correct direction.
5. f you are passing through wide open area with hardly discernible paths, please pay attention to the opposite side edge of canopy in case there is a big belt-shaped marking (so-called "tout").

6. There are cases when the rules of marking or the prescribed 3-year interval of renovation of marking were not observed. It can cause poor legibility, insufficient frequency or discrepancy of the marking with regards to the map. Drawbacks are also caused by ploughing away the field roads, building of fences or new forest roads.
7. Look back from time to time and observe the marking running in the opposite direction. It may be more reliable.
8. It is recommendable to measure the distance quoted in the map if you want to calculate the time of the trip and its length.
9. The data on road posts contain information on distances (the first line of the chart quotes the nearest point with road post on the trail, the second and third line inform about important places on the route and the last line quotes the end point).
10. The marked hiking trails are fully utilizable only if there is no snow cover.

Maps

Every route is accompanied by a map with the course of the route. In spite of it, it is recommendable to carry a detailed map issued by VKÚ Harmanec. Particularly, we recommend the series of maps at scale 1:25 000: No. 1 Nízke Tatry — rekreačné strediská, No. 2 Vysoké Tatry — Starý Smokovec, No. 3 Západné Tatry — Podbanské — Zverovka, No. 4 Slovenský raj, No. 6 Donovaly — Šachtička — Turecká, and No. 7 Pieniny.

Transport

The area of the northern Slovakia boasts comparatively thick network of bus lines and in some cases also railway lines. The starting and finishing points of the individual routes are accessible by the collective means of transport. It means that each tour (with the exception of the trips starting and ending at high-mountain cottages or hotels) can be accomplished by going to its starting point by bus or train. The same is applicable with regards to the finishing point.

The ridge of the Západné Tatry Mts.

Situation

The mountain range of Západné Tatry spreads between the 49°09' and 49°17' of northern geographic latitude and 19°34' and 20°01' of eastern geographical longitude. The range lies on a rectangular area, one side of which is more than 30 km and the other 16 km long. Its southern limit where the area borders on the deeply cut-in Liptovská kotlina basin is the most contrasting one. The southern foothill line is well-visible and it runs between Podbanské on the east and Liptovské Matiašovce in the west. The Západné Tatry Mts. neighbour with Chočské vrchy Mts. in the west. Both ranges are separated after a short spur of Holice (1,339 m). The range also borders on a depression in the north. This depression is shallower and narrower than the Liptovská kotlina basin in the south. The Západné Tatry Mts. is skirted here by the westernmost part of Podtatranská brázda furrow called the Zuberecká brázda furrow. It continues into the territory of Poland. The High Tatras lie in the east of the Západné Tatry Mts. The border between them leads from the Ľaliové sedlo saddle (1,947 m) in the main ridge over the back part of the Tichá dolina valley to the Závory saddle (1,879 m) in the side ridge of the Liptovské kopy Mts. Passing through the Závory saddle it drops to the bottom of

9

Below the Baranec Mt.

the Kôprová dolina valley and continues following its axis as far as Podbanské on the southern foothill of the range.

The Západné Tatry Mts. became the frontier mountain massif between the historic territories of Hungary and Poland already in the Middle Ages. They separated the Slovak Orava and the Polish region of Podhale in the north and the regions of Orava and Liptov in the south. The range maintained its historic role of an important and distinct natural frontier. It lies in the north of the central part of Slovakia on the frontier with Poland. Poland possesses approximately one third of the territory of the range, the rest is Slovak. The Slovak-Polish frontier runs along the main ridge of the Západné Tatry between the Ľaliové sedlo saddle (1,947 m) in the east and Volovec Mt. (2,063 m) in the west. The frontier leaves the Volovec Mt. to turn to the north and tracing the lateral ridge of Rákoň it drops as far as the northern edge of the range. The new territorial division of Slovakia, which entered in force in 1996, included the whole territory of the Západné Tatry Mts. into the province of Žilina. Only a small eastern part of it is now under the district of Poprad, province of Prešov. The north-western part of the Západné Tatry Mts. reaches as far as Tvrdošín and some of its parts stretching south of the main ridge are lying on the territory of the district of Liptovský Mikuláš.

Natural setting

Substratum and surface

The geological picture of the Západné Tatry Mts. is very similar to that of Východné or Vysoké Tatry mountain ranges. Both are classified as crystalline-Mesozoic mountain ranges of the Western Carpathians, part of them consists of igneous rocks and transformed rocks by crystallisation and another part of them forms a belt of sediments of the Mesozoic sea. They differ in two aspects. The first of them concerns the crystalline part of the massif and the second is in the sedimentary belt in the north. Deep igneous material of granite type dominates in the High Tatras while schist prevails in the Západné Tatry Mts. The Mesozoic sediments, prevailingly dolomite and limestone, represent a minor role in the Vysoké Tatry forming a narrow belt on the northern foothills of the range. This belt becomes wider only in the Belianske Tatry Mts. The width of this sedimentary belt increases in Západné Tatry Mts. to such an extent that it reaches the main ridge of the Červené vrchy Mts. Besides, dolomite and limestone occur more frequently in the north-western and western parts of the range, where they continue to the west, up to the Chočské vrchy Mts.

Sivý vrch Mt.

Dinosaur from the Tichá dolina valley

The couple of Slovak geologists working in the Tichá dolina valley in the eastern part of the Západné Tatry Mts. packed in their bag a piece of rock bearing unusual imprints. Laboratory analysis showed that the little hollows on the surface of the sandstone were in fact the footprints of a bulky three-digit creature. Palaeontologists found out that the creature treading the primeval Tichá dolina valley was a kind of dinosaur with scientific name of Coelurosaurichus tatricus. The traces of this saurian were conserved on surface of sandstone, which was soft mud about 195 million years ago. The experts suppose that what later became the Tatras was undergoing the Alpine folding, which preceded the origin of the Mesozoic folding mountain range. The area of the present Tichá dolina valley was presumably a glowing wasteland with scattered tropic vegetation. The sandy mud dried, hardened after some time and finally turned into sandstone conserving the footprints of the primeval fauna of the Tatras.

Gigantic relief forming processes followed the sedimentation of rocks in

Relaxation below the main ridge

the Mesozoic Sea. Bulky layers of rocks folded and displaced to comparatively long distances in form of huge mantles. This mountain range formed at the end of the Mesozoic era was very different from what we know as the Tatras today. Its appearance and altitude can be only imagined because water and wind later reduced it. Gradual disappearance of the Tatra landscape about 70 million years ago reached the stage, when the former and considerably denuded mountain ridges sank under the water table of the Tertiary Sea and remained hidden under thick layers of sea sediments. The regularly alternating layers of sandstone and claystone called Flysch are to be seen in the filling of the sub Tatra basins. The present appearance of the Tatra started to form about 15 to 20 million years ago. First it was low middle mountain range lacking tall rock crests and deep valleys, which we can admire there now in the Západné but above in the High Tatras

The decisive changes, which endowed the Západné Tatry Mts. its present attractive form, took place in the last two million years. They were caused by tectonic movements abundantly assisted by eroding valley glaciers. The inner forces acting beneath the range uplifted it above the surrounding basins and furrows to such an extent that they reached the permanent snow line in the glacial era. This important climatic frontier ran at

The peaks of the Západné Tatry Mts. taller than 2,000 m a.s.l.

1.	Bystrá	2,248.4	16.	Malolučniak	2,104.8
2.	Jakubina	2,193.7	17.	Temniak	2,096.3
3.	Baranec	2,184.0	18.	Vyšná Magura	2,095.2
4.	Baníkov	2,178.0	19.	Ostrý Roháč	2,087.5
5.	Klin	2,172.7	20.	Spálená	2,083.3
6.	Pachoľa	2,166.6	21.	Smrek	2,071.9
7.	Hrubá kopa	2,166.4	22.	Smrečiny	2,068.2
8.	Nižná Bystrá	2,162.3	23.	Volovec	2,063.4
9.	Blyšť	2,154.7	24.	Veľká kopa	2,052.4
10.	Príslop	2,141.9	25.	Nohavica	2,051.7
11.	Hrubý vrch	2,136.9	26.	Ostredok	2,049.7
12.	Tri kopy	2,136.3	27.	Salatín	2,047.5
13.	Veľká Kamenistá	2,127.4	28.	Ježová	2,043.2
14.	Plačlivé	2,124.5	29.	Kondratova kopa	2,004.6
15.	Kresanica	2,121.9			

the approximate altitude above sea level of 1,400-1,500 m in the last glacial era called Wurm by the experts. If the relief of the range rose to the altitude of 3,000 m it would also be the altitude of the present climatic frontier. Glaciers repeatedly filled the valleys of the Západné Tatry in the Quaternary Age and the mountain ridges changed into inhospitable and harsh tundra or freezing stone desert. Total 13 independent glaciers, 5 on the northern and 8 on the southern side of the Slovak part of the mountain range originated. The bulkiest glacier formed in Kôprová dolina valley on the eastern edge of the Západné Tatry Mts. It was 9 km long and 200 m thick. The glacier tongues in the Roháčska, Jačkova, and Žiarska dolina valleys were comparable to the High Tatry valley glaciers. All glaciers in the Západné Tatry Mts. thawed at the beginning of the Holocene era, about 8.5 thousand years ago leaving here the typical glacier relief with cirques, troughs and several glacier lakes. Erosion activity of the disappeared glaciers is also evidenced by several scratched rock protuberances called in scientific language *rouche moutoneé*.

The Západné Tatry Mts. along with the Východné Tatry Mts. (including the ranges of the Vysoké and Belianske Tatry) form a geomorphologic whole, which is classified among the mountain ranges of the Fatransko-tatranská region of the Inner Western Carpathians. The Západné Tatry stand for a quieter western neighbour to the higher and more visited the High Tatras in the east. The northern mountain rim of Liptovská kotlina basin continues by the Chočské vrchy Mts. which are shorter in their easternmost part by about 500 m than the peaks of the westernmost part of the Západné Tatry Mts. In the south the mountain range borders on deeply cut in Liptovská

Holý vrch Mt.

kotlina basin, which is the western unit of the Podtatranská kotlina basin. In spite of the fact that it is the highest situated basin of the Western Carpathians, they are taller by 1,700 m. The narrow Zuberecká brázda furrow, which represents the western part of the elongated Podtatranská brázda furrow lies on the northern side of the mountain range. Its eastern end reaches as far as the village Ždiar lying below the Belianske Tatry Mts. This depression is about 100 m higher situated than the Liptovská kotlina basin on the opposite side of the mountain range. The Zuberecká brázda furrow borders in the north with relatively short and round ridges of the Skorušinské vrchy Mts. with sea level altitude slightly over 1,300 m. This also is the reason why looking from the north, the Západné Tatry Mts. look so monumental and create a bulky background of the picturesque Orava landscape.

The Západné Tatry Mts. with its maximum altitude above sea level 2,248 is the second to the tallest mountain range in Slovakia. Only the High Tatras are taller by 400 metres. The Západné Tatry Mts. also occupy an important position within the framework of the whole Carpathian Arch ranking among the ten highest mountain ranges. Apart from the High Tatras six mountain massifs of the Southern and Eastern Carpathians in Romania are taller, while all Ukrainian Carpathian mountain ranges are shorter. There are 29 two thousand meter or more tall peaks in the Západné Tatry Mts. including its tallest Bystrá Mt. in its eastern part.

The **main ridge** of the Západné Tatry Mts. runs approximately along the line of the geographic parallel. It is 37 km long and winding. Its westernmost peak is the Biela skala Mt. (1,316 m) towering above the Hutianske sedlo saddle. The ridge ends in the east by the often visited Kasprov vrch Mt. (1,985 m). In the central ridge of the Západné Tatry Mts. there are 27 mountains and 20 of them are taller than 2,000 m. Their mean height is 2,035 m. The tallest peak of the main ridge is Baníkov (2,178 m) in the Roháče Mts. Kresanica Mt. (2,122 m) is the tallest peak of its eastern part. The most conspicuous low points of the main ridge of the Západné Tatry Mts. are the saddles Pálenica (1,573 m) and Tomanovské sedlo (1,686 m). The remaining saddles seldom drop under 1,900 m above sea level.

The main ridge has several **lateral ridges** protruding north and southward. Seen from the west on the southern side are the ridges of Babky (1,565 m), Ráztoky (1,948 m), Baranec (2,184 m), Jakubina (2,194 m), Bystrá (2,248 m) and Liptovské kopy (2,052 m). Asymmetrical uplifting of the Tatras is the cause why their peaks are taller than all peaks of the main ridge. The southern lateral ridges drop abruptly by 1,000 m to 1,500 m. The Liptovské kopy Mts. represent the separate mountain group situated on the east of the southern slops of the Západné Tatry Mts. They are separated from the surrounding landscape by a ring of the Tichá and Kôprová dolina valleys. This concave massif sharply

Passage over the ridge

contrasts with the adjacent majestic Kriváň Mt. in the High Tatras. The northern lateral ridges are longer and not so tall. The bulky group of Osobitá (1,678 m), the lateral branch of the forked lateral bridge Rákoň (1,663 m) are dominating there. The second branch traces the Slovak-Polish frontier and culminates in the Bobrovec Mt. (1,663 m). The slopes of the remaining northern lateral ridges east of the Volovec Mt. (2,063 m) are dropping to the Polish side of the Západné Tatry Mts.

The lateral ridges on the southern side of the Západné Tatry Mts. regularly alternate with the little branched Žiarska dolina valley, the twin valleys of Jamnícka and Račkova, as well as the Bystrá dolina valley, which as the only one does not reach as far as the main ridge. The two most beautiful and largest **valleys** lie in the east. They are the Tichá and Kôprová valleys. The northern valleys of the Slovak part of the Západné Tatry Mts. are arranged in a different way. There is only one large and branched Roháčska dolina valley. The attractive valleys of Bobrovecká and Juráňová are situated under the lateral ridge of the Bobrovec Mt. and run to the north to the Podtatranská brázda furrow. The Juráňov potok brook has modelled there a narrow and picturesque gorge in resistant limestone and dolomite rocks. The Západné Tatry Mts. or the Western Tatras were called Liptovské hole or sim-

In the Račkova dolina valley

ply Hole. The older name suited them better (hole means mountains covered with alpine meadows) because they differ from the rocks prevailing in the eastern Tatras. The alpine meadows often reach as far as the tips of the tallest peaks. Only the Roháče Mts. or the limestone-dolomite massif of the Sivý vrch Mt., the Osobitá and the Červené vrchy in the easternmost section of the main ridge are the typical denuded rocks. **Roháče** are often and justly praised as the most beautiful part of the Západné Tatry Mts. A crown of wonderful peaks dominated by the majestic Baníkov Mt. surrounds the extensive Roháčska dolina valley. In turn, the Ostrý Roháč and Volovec Mts. are the princes of the Roháče Mts. They form an indivisible couple of slender rock mountains in the principal ridge and look like two devil's horns, expressed by their names (Ostrý Roháč means sharp horn and Volovec means ox).

The red on white

The Červené vrchy Mts. (in English The Red Mountains) derive their name from the grass growing on their tops coloured in red after the early autumn frost burn it. Maybe, if there was no vegetation their name would be the White Mountains, because under the grass on the northern slopes of the upper part of the Tichá dolina valley is the white limestone rock, which forms the typical step-like rock galleries. The limestone of the Červené vrchy Mts. is the substratum suitable for the origin of surface and underground karstic phenomena or caves in common language. It is the highest situated karstic area in Slovakia.

There is also the highest situated sinkhole in the Červené vrchy Mts. immediately below the top of the Kresanica Mt. in the altitude of about 2,000 m above sea level. The Slovak altitude record is also the abyss of Vyšná Kresanica located at the height 2,081 m. There are also other chimney-like abysses nearby: Zadný úplaz 82 m deep, Kresanica with the bottom 71 m below the terrain and Laďová priepasť abyss, which is 11 m shallower. The Nová Kresanica cave 550 m long is in turn the highest situated cave in Slovakia with its entrance at 2,000 m above sea level. There are lapies fields on the slopes of Kresanica the same as in the Rozpadlá dolina valley where there is also a karstic spring yielding an average of 80 litres of water per second. Even richer high-mountain karst can be admired on the Polish side of the Červené vrchy Mts. The limestone of the Sivý vrch massif, Osobitá Mt., Juráňová dolina valley and in the environs of the gamekeeper's lodge of Brestová in the Západné Tatry Mts. also karstificated. Right within the ridge of the Sivý vrch is the deepest Tatra abyss with its bottom in the depth of 88 m. This mountain is adorned by awe inspiring rock forms with split limestone-dolomite towers. Under the Biela skala rock not far away are the underground corridors, known by the local people as the Baňaryho štôlňa gallery. Next to the gamekeeper's lodge Brestová in the Roháčska dolina valley is the entrance to the Brestovská jaskyňa cave, the longest in the Západné Tatry Mts. It is 1,450 m long. Bones of a long extinct cave bear were found in the Medvedia jaskyňa cave in the Suchá dolina valley.

Climate and waters

The climate of the Západné Tatry Mts. is determined, apart from the geographical position, by altitude. The climate is divided into altitude steps starting by warmer and favourable parameters at the foothill of the range and ending by extremely inhospitable cold and humid high-mountain conditions on high and windy summits. The summers are cold and rainy with mean July temperatures under 16° Celsius at the foothills and well-below 10° Celsius over the upper timber line. In summer months frequent thunderstorms accompanied by sudden weather changes, which can bring snow in high mountains even in the middle of summer are not rare. The most stable weather can be counted on in autumn. The period of what is called the Indian summer (end of September and October) is characterized by cold but lasting sunny weather. The only disadvantage of the autumn high-mountain hiking are the short days. The winters in the Západné Tatry Mts. are very cold and rich in snow. The mean temperatures in lower positions drop to 5°

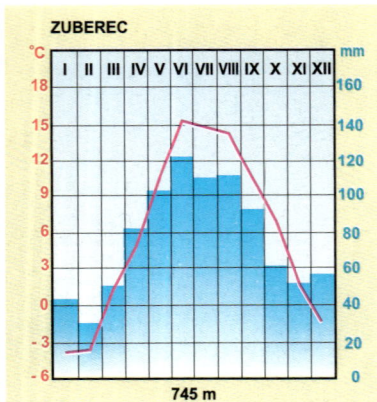

ZUBEREC

745 m

Monthly temperatures and precipitation

Celsius below zero in January, they are even lower at the summits, 10° Celsius below zero. The Západné Tatry Mts. is the most humid region of Slovakia. Snow cover lasts as much as 200 days a year. Snow fields sometimes last until the beginning of summer. A frequent and dangerous phenomenon in the Západné Tatry Mts. are the snow avalanches falling down the smooth slopes. Humid air mass is coming normally from the north-west as the crests of the Beskydy Mts. in Poland are too low to prevent it. Only the tall ridge of the Západné Tatry Mts., which cast what is called the precipitation shadow to the Liptov side of the range stops them. Thanks to it the Liptov region is dryer than Orava region. The Západné Tatry Mts. represent an important hydrographic divide as the **main European water divide** runs along its ridges. It is interesting that this important border between two European river systems coincides with the Polish-Slovak frontier. The whole Polish side of the mountain range is in the basin of the Dunajec, which drains the water through the Visla to the Baltic Sea. The Slovak part of the Západné Tatry Mts. is part of the Váh basins and its right tributary Orava, the water of which flows through the Danube to the Black Sea. The greatest **water stream** of the

The twelve largest lakes in the Západné Tatry Mts.

	Area in hectares	Altitude above see level in m
1. Prvé Roháčske pleso	2.22	1,562
2. Štvrté Roháčske pleso	1.45	1,719
3. Nižné Jamnícke pleso	1.18	1,728
4. Vyšné Bystré pleso	0.85	1,878
5. Vyšné Račkovo pleso	0.74	1,717
6. Tretie Roháčske pleso	0.61	1,653
7. Vyšné Jamnícke pleso	0.41	1,834
8. Anitino očko	0.34	1,837
9. Pleso pod Zverovkou	0.31	963
10. Ťatliakovo jazero	0.28	1,370
11. Druhé Roháčske pleso	0.28	1,650
12. Nižné Tomanovské pleso	0.19	1,592

Orava part of the mountain range, which lies north of the main ridge is the Studený potok flowing in the huge Roháčska dolina valley. The Studený potok brook unifies the network of brooks in the north-west in the mountain range. The Bobrovecký and Juráňov potok brooks are exceptions. They join in Oravice and flow across the Skorušinské vrchy Mts. to the north and to the Oravská kotlina basin as the Oravice brook. The brooks on the Liptov side of the Západné Tatry Mts. with few exceptions do not join in the mountain range or in the Liptovská kotlina basin. They independently mouth into the Váh. One of the

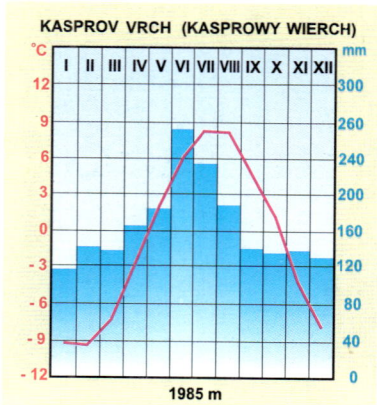

KASPROV VRCH (KASPROWY WIERCH)

Monthly temperatures and precipitation

exceptions is the Jamnícky potok and Račková brooks flowing through the valleys bearing the same name. The greatest brook of the range is the east: the Tichý potok brook in the 14 km long valley of the same name. After it joins the Kôprovský potok brook near Podbanské it acquires the name Belá. The brooks of the Západné Tatry Mts. are torrential, they reach the highest discharges in spring when snow thaws. Studený potok brook has a mean annual discharge of 3.7 cubic metres per second. Average annual discharge of 3.8 cubic metres per second was measured on the Belá brook. The inclination of the valleys is not even and this gave origin to **waterfalls**. The Roháčsky vodopád waterfall below the Roháčske plesá lakes is the highest and the best known of them. On the slope of the Spálená dolina valley the water falls over a rock threshold from the height of 18 m, there also are smaller waterfalls, such as the Šarafiov vodopád waterfall in the Žiarska dolina valley and the Tomanovský vodopád waterfall in Tomanovská the dolina valley.

About 20 small **glacier lakes** survive in the Západné Tatry Mts. The largest of them is the Prvé Roháčske pleso lake with an area of 2,22 ha and the deepest is the Vyšné Račkovo pleso lake in the Račkova dolina valley (10 m). The Vyšné Bystré pleso lake is the highest situated of the permanent lakes. Its water table is at 1,876 m above sea level. Lower situated lakes are the water bodies, which originated after moraines blocked the water here. The origin of the Pleso pod Zverovkou lake is specific because it originated, like the Štrbské pleso lake in the High Tatras, by thawing of the ice inside the moraine material. All lakes in the Tatras are gradually disappearing.

The view of the ridge of the Západné Tatry Mts.

Their "slow death" is caused by silting and progressive change into peat bogs. Their disappearance is imminent, their areas are diminishing and this is the reason why the data on the area of the largest lakes of the Západné Tatry Mts. are not reliable.

Soil, vegetation and wild life

The **soil cover** in the territory of the Západné Tatry Mts. varies depending on climate, relief parameters and properties of the geological substratum. The altitude zones manifest both in climate and vegetation. The noncarbonate soil prevails on the crystalline rocks, while on the slopes of the range, which are built by the Mesozoic sediments the carbonate soils, such as rendzinas are more abundant. Generally the forest and high-mountain soil classes and types dominate. Agricultural soil inside the mountain range is substantially less represented than in the Liptovská kotlina basin or Zuberecká brázda furrow. The most frequent types of soil are podzols and rendzinas on the forested slopes of the range. Gleyic soils linked to peat bogs originated on waterlogged areas.

From the phytogeographic point of view the territory of the Západné Tatry Mts. is in the area of the Western Carpathian flora. The larger part of it is in the district of Eastern Beskydy flora, only a small area near Oravice is classified into the district of the Western Beskydy flora. **Vegetation** of the range is arranged into several altitude vegetation steps while the forest plant associations prevail. The lower part of the slopes on the edge of it, approximately to the altitude of 700 m above sea level lie in the sub-mountain altitude step. Originally, there existed numerous peat bogs, which were considerably reduced by melioration. Higher, up to the altitude 1,250 m above sea level is the mountain vegetation step. The lower slopes of these steps were covered by beach stands, mixed firs and spruces in the past. But they were severely affected by grazing, charcoal production or they were substituted by spruces. Spruce steps reached as high as the upper timber line in the Západné Tatry Mts. Spruce stands represent the most spread type of forest in these parts. On the slopes covered by continuous debris fields are the ash-maple forests. Pines are less represented. The **upper timber line** is an important natural frontier in the Západné Tatry Mts. Originally it reached the altitude 1,500 m above sea level, but the cattle and sheep shepherds artificially lowered it by about 100, 150 metres through burning and clearing. A comparatively extensive mountain dwarf pine vegetation step is above the upper timber line. They used to be even more extensive in the past, but sheep keeping destroyed large areas of this wood species. In the course of 400 years as much as 60 percent of dwarf pine stands was substituted by pastures. Although this unfavourable development was stopped in recent decades, today the dwarf pine step completely absents in places and it is replaced by meadows often stricken by snow avalanches and severe soil erosion. In experts' opinion the smooth slopes of the Západné Tatry Mts. are more prone to avalanches than the High Tatras. Statistics confirm it.

The El Dorado of shepherds

Shepherds manifested great interest in the Západné Tatry Mts. as early as in time of the Wallachian colonisation in the 16th century. The old footpaths of shepherds called here vandrovky ran along the brooks and headed into the valleys at the beginning. However, the lower situated pastures to which these footpaths led were soon exhausted and the shepherds had to drive their herds to ever higher positions. Vandrovky were becoming longer and some of them were as much as 18 kilometres long. The sheep-keeping activity in the Západné Tatry Mts. culminated at the turn of the 16th and 17th centuries.

At that time forty-one villages of the Orava and Liptov regions had 136 sheilings or sheep farms with hundreds of sheep and cattle on the alpine meadows of the Západné Tatry Mts. Shepherds from Poland also had their animals grazing in the area. Sheep-farming in the Západné Tatry Mts. disappeared by the end of the 1970's while in the 1950's, for instance, 1,060 sheep and 200 cows were still grazing in the area of the Tichá dolina valley. When the Tatra National Park was founded the number of sheep grazing in the area of the protected territory was very limited.

In the altitude of 1,800 m above sea level and higher is the alpine vegetation step. Herb associations with higher portion of sporophytes (lichens, algae and mosses) survive here in harsh high-mountain environment on show fields, rock faces, fissures and faults or on natural alpine meadows. Plant vegetation is varied especially in the areas with carbonate substratum. Several rare plant species, which do not grow anywhere else in Slovakia, live in the Západné Tatry Mts.: clover, burr reed or *Sparganium aungustifolium*, *Sibbaldia procumbens*, alpine toad flax or *Linaria alpine*, and sedge (*Carex*). Glacial relics such as the dryad and *Arctous alpine* are typical for the high-mountain environment.

The **wild life** of the Západné Tatry Mts. is also varied and abundant. Cosmopolitan, European, Palaeo-arctic species and endemites are represented here. The mountain vegetation step is the most populated one by fauna and the most rare species are found in the high-mountain landscape above the upper timber line. The amphibians have their representative in two species of newt (*Triturus montandori*) and the endemite *Triturus alpestris*. Birds include *Prunella collaris* nesting around Zuberec and *Tichodroma muraria*, which inhabits the high-situated alpine meadows. The black stark nests around Oravice. The wolf, fox, bear, boar, reed-deer and herds of chamois pasturing in the high situated meadows are also at home here.

Nature conservation

The territory of the Západné Tatry Mts. is now part of the **TANAP** (The Tatra National Park) established in 1949 as the first National Park in Slovakia. The territory was first part of its protective zone and later it was integrated into the proper territory of the TANAP by the Resolution of the Government of the Slovak Republic No 12 of April 1987. The Západné Tatry Mts. with its area 29,324 ha represent 38 percent of the total area of the TANAP (75,405 ha). A stricter protection regime is applied to the **small protected areas**, seventeen (ten national nature reserves, 3 nature reserves 1 national nature phenomenon and 1 nature phenomenon) in the territory of the Západné Tatry Mts. The Tichá dolina valley is the largest national nature reserve since 1991 on an area 5,967 ha. The oldest small protected area in the Západné Tatry Mts. is the Kotlový žľab trough in the Látaná dolina valley established as early as 1934 with the aim to protect the rare primeval forest vegetation. Today it is the national nature reserve on an area of 70.8 ha.

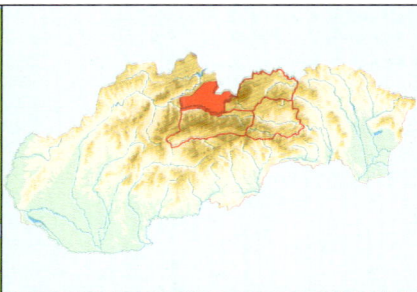

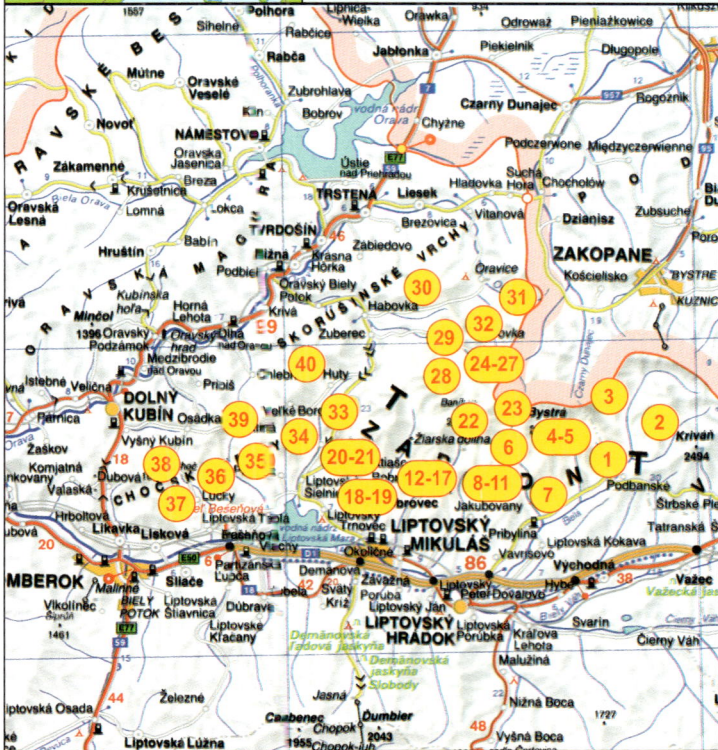

1 Around Podbanské

Podbanské – Kôprová dolina – Pod Grúnikom – Tri studničky – Podbanské

Situation: The Západné Tatry Mts. – South (eastern part).
Starting and finishing point: Podbanské – recreation village, bus stop, parking lot.
Time schedule: Podbanské - Tichá ½ h –

Pod Grúnikom 1 h – Tri studničky ¾ h – Podbanské 1 ¾ h.
Total: 4 hours.
Elevation gain: 300 m.
Map: Západné Tatry – Roháče 1 : 50 000 (sheet 112), VKÚ, š. p., Harmanec.

Classification: Easy, little demanding half-day tour.
Basic route: Start next to the bus stop below Podbanské and continue up the main road to the turning to **Podbanské** (950 m). In the lower part of the parking lot is a map and a road post. Follow the yellow and red-marked footpath turning right onto the main road, cross the little bridge over the Belá river and continue to the crossroads with road post indicating the direction to the Tichá dolina valley. Turn left and continue on asphalt road marked in yellow (8851) and you will reach the crossroads near the **Tichá gamekeeper's house** (983 m) in about 30 minutes. There is a shelter, road post, a monument to the heroes of the Slovak National Uprising, and information boards for cyclists. Turn right and continue following the green mark (5802) and ascend on asphalt road by the gamekeeper's house. After a while turn slightly left and continue through beautiful spruce forest. The forest will soon open and you will be able to see the Kriváň Mt. (2,494 m). After an hour you will arrive at the **crossroads Pod Grúnikom** (1,104 m). The Kôprova dolina valley is seasonally closed. Continue ascending the blue-marked path (2902) below the steep slopes of the Grúnik Mt. and through spruce forest. Still ascending you will have to turn left along a long curve and then right onto the crest of the Veľká Pálenica Mt. up to

Podbanské

the altitude of 1,250 m above sea level, which is the highest point of the tour. Start descending passing through a romantic meadow with a splendid view of the Kriváň Mt. Walking on the forest road you will cross a wide vertical draining channel and descend to the alpine meadow above Tri studničky. The footpath running along the edge of the forest joins the green-marked path to the Kriváň Mt. (5803). A road post, large shelter and a spring are at the forest edge. You are in the little settlement of forest workers called **Tri studničky** (1,141 m). This is where you enter the red-marked main Tatra hiking trail called here "magistrála" (0930). Continue down the road passing by the gamekeeper's lodge and turn off the road before arriving at the crossroads through a steep little meadow to the forest onto a dug out path. Now you traverse the lateral ridges of the Veľká Pálenica Mt. in moderate ascents and descents. The route continues slightly to the right, then down on a wide road and slightly descending it arrives at the crossroads of forest roads. Continue straight ahead on the forest road, and then slightly to the left until you arrive at the meadow of Nadbanské. Walking on the edge of the meadow you will get onto asphalt road and continue along the buildings of forest management slightly to the left. Turn right down to the crossroads to the Tichá dolina valley and onto the main road. After crossing over the Belá river you will arrive at **Podbanské**.

2 Around the Liptovské kopy Mts.

Podbanské – Kôprová dolina – Závory – Tichá dolina – Podbanské

Situation: The Západné Tatry Mts. – South (eastern part).
Starting and finishing point: Podbanské – recreation village, bus stop, parking lot.
Time schedule: Podbanské – Tichá ½ h – Pod Grúnikom 1 h – Pod Hlinskou dolinou 2 h – Pod Temnými smrečinami ¼ h – Závory 1 ¼ h – Pod Tomanovou 2 h – Tichá 2 ¾ h – Podbanské ½ h.
Total: 10 ¼ hours.
Elevation gain: 929 m.
Map: Západné Tatry – Roháče 1 : 50 000 (sheet 112), VKÚ, š. p., Harmanec.

Classification: The tour is demanding for its length.
Basic route: This route will carry you to the deepest valleys of the easternmost part of the Západné Tatry Mts. Start at the bus stop below Podbanské and then carry on through **Podbanské** (950 m), crossroads next to the **gamekeeper' lodge Tichá** (983 m). This tour agrees with the route No. 1 up to the **crossroads Pod Grúnikom** (1,104 m). Continue on blue mark (2902) over the bridge and on the left side of the brook up the **Kôprová dolina valley**. You are walking on asphalt road and you can admire the deep troughs of the Kriváň Mt. on your right and the round Liptovské kopy Mts. on the other side. After about an hour walk you can hear the roar of the highest (80 m) Tatra waterfall, the **Kmeťov vodopád waterfall** where the asphalt road ends. Now you are drawing closer to the Nefcerka valley with a 5 minute detour to the waterfalls. After seeing the waterfall return to the original route and the asphalt road gradually changes into a rocky path leading through the forest and clearings to the **crossroads Pod Hlinskou dolinou.** The path joins again the green mark (5801). After a 15 minute walk in forest you will get to a waterlogged meadow. The paths are fixed with logs here. Now you are at the **crossroads** called **Pod Temnými smrečinami.** The red-marked path on your right turns off to two Temnosmrečianske plesá lakes passing by the Vajanský vodopád waterfall. But you will continue to the left of the road post from the meadow through an ever thinner forest to the belt of dwarf pine forest. Ascending on winding path through a grassy slope you

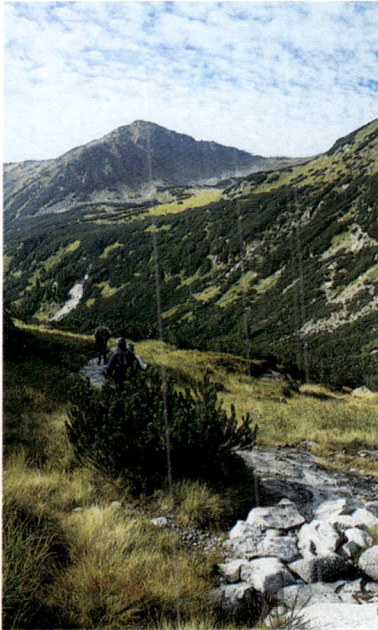

Sedlo Závory saddle

will get to the little plain of the Kobylia dolina valley with the Kobylie pleso lake (1,742 m) about 150 m away on the right side of the footpath. Proceeding in beautiful meadows with alpine flora and later up a steep slope, you will eventually reach the **Závory saddle** (1,879 m). The award for the toilsome ascent will be soon obvious in form of fine view of the Temné smrečiny with the Čubrina Mt., the crest of the Kriváň Mt., the Červené vrchy Mts., and the ridges of the Západné Tatry and Vysoké Tatry mountain ranges. The descent from the Závory saddle leads along the red-marked path (0931) through the Zadná Tichá dolina valley and below the Garajove kopy Mts. At the beginning you will descend down the steep grassy slope with attractive views of the side valleys of Temná Tichá and Zadné Licierovo. Later crossing a dwarf pine forest you will enter a thin forest and gravel road. On your right you are passing by the head of the Kamenná Tichá dolina valley. After about 15 minute walk you will arrive at a shelter where asphalt road starts. There is about 300 metres to a road post with red-marked turning to the Suché sedlo saddle. Cross the bridge to the left bank of the brook and in 30 minutes you will reach the **Pod Tomanovou crossroads** (1,166 m). The red-marked path turns to the Tomanovské sedlo saddle (1,686 m) here. Continue on the left bank of the brook following the yellow mark (8851) first passing by the Rakytový žľab trough and then the Špania dolina valley. Snow avalanches threaten almost all troughs in this valley. There are numerous cottages, a monument to the heroes of the Slovak National Uprising on a large meadow. You are now descending down a moderately inclined valley up to the **gamekeeper's lodge Tichá**. A thirty minute walk will bring you to **Podbanské**.

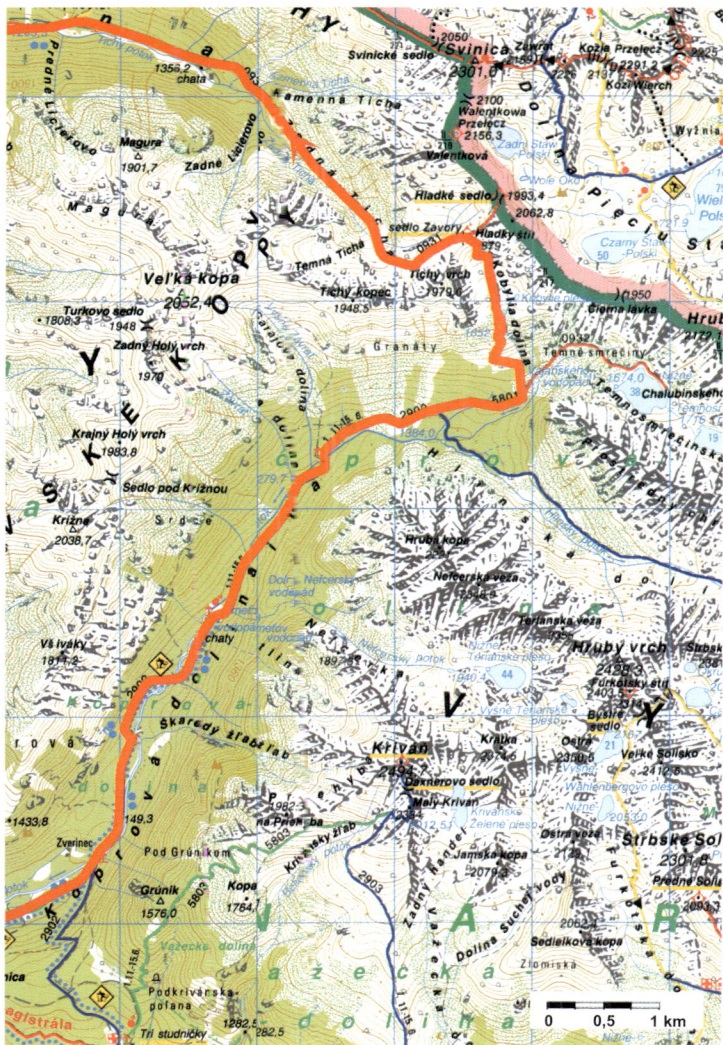

3 To the Tomanovské sedlo saddle

Podbanské – Tichá dolina – Tomanovské sedlo – Tichá dolina – Podbanské

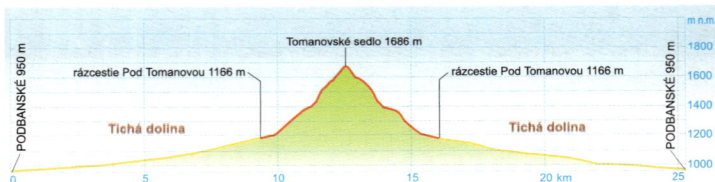

Situation: The Západné Tatry Mts. – South (eastern part).
Starting and finishing point: Podbanské – recreation village, bus stop, parking lot.
Time schedule: Podbanské – Tichá ½ h –

Pod Tomanovou 2 ¾ h – Tomanovské sedlo 1 ½ h – Podbanské 4 h.
Total: 8 ¾ hours.
Elevation gain: 736 m.
Map: Západné Tatry – Roháče 1 : 50 000 (sheet 112), VKÚ, š. p., Harmanec.

Classification: Moderately difficult, comparatively long trip.
Basic route: Start at the bus stop below the Podbanské continue through **Podbanské** (950 m) and the route coincides with the route No. 1 up to the crossroads near the Tichá gamekeeper's lodge. At the crossroads turn left, cross the bridge over the Kôprovský potok brook, go on along a log gamekeeper's lodge slightly descending to a large meadow. Here you will get the first opportunity to see the enormous dimensions of the **Tichá dolina valley** with its side valleys. After a moderate ascent through the valley the lateral Kôprovnica valley enters the Tichá dolina valley on the right while the large valley dolina Hlina appears later on your left. After about a two hour walk from the crossroads of the Tichá gamekeeper's lodge you will arrive at a large meadow with log buildings and a monument to the heroes of the Slovak National Uprising. This place is referred to as "Tábor" (The Camp) and there is the seasonal closure of the tourist route. Avalanche troughs skirt the following stretch of the road on both sides and after about 45 minutes you will reach the **crossroads** called **Pod Tomanovou** (1,166 m). Turn onto the red-marked path (0931) next to the road post in the direction to the Tomanovská dolina valley. Cross the Tichý and Tomanovský potok brooks and you will arrive at a shelter next to about seven meters high **Tomanovský vodopád waterfall** below the road. Continue ahead up to the Javorový žľab trough and later over the brook to the left below the Rozpad-

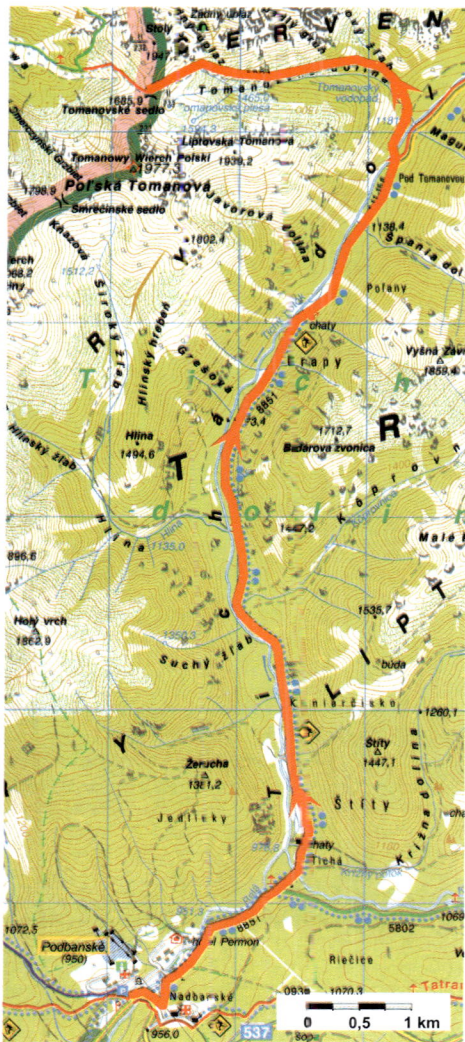

nutý grúň slope to the Tomanovská dolina valley. Now you are crossing a thin forest ascending to the dwarf pine zone and further to glacier kettle. The ascent becomes milder but only for a while as the end part becomes ever steeper on the grassy slope of the summit of the Stoly Mt. and the **Tomanovské sedlo saddle** (1,686 m) next to the Polish frontier. You can see the Tomanovské plesá lakes, which is being gradually overgrown by peat, the massive Tomanová Mountain and the ridges of the Vysoké and Západné Tatry mountain ranges. You can return taking the original route of ascent.

4 Across the Blyšť Mt. to the Račkova dolina valley

Podbanské – Kamenistá dolina – Blyšť – Klin – Račkovo sedlo – end of Račkova dolina

Situation: The Západné Tatry Mts. – South (eastern part).

Starting point: Podbanské – recreation village, bus stop, parking lot.

Finishing point: End of Račkova dolina, car-camping site, bus stop, parking lot.

Time schedule: Podbanské – Kamenistá dolina ¼ h – Pyšné sedlo 3 h – Blyšť ¾ h – Bystré sedlo ½ h – Gáborovo sedlo ¼ h – Klin ¾ h – Račkovo sedlo ½ h – end of Račkova dolina 2 ¾ h.

Total: 8 ¾ hours.

Elevation gain: 1,283 m.

Map: Západné Tatry – Roháče 1 : 50 000 (sheet 112), VKÚ, š. p., Harmanec.

Classification: Medium difficult and comparatively long tour with steep ascents and descents.

Basic route: Start at the bus stop near Podbanské and continue up the main road to the turning to **Podbanské** (950). In the lower part of the parking lot is a road pole and a map. Choose the blue-marked path (2901), which runs along with the red-marked main Tatra hiking route slightly to the right and upwards. Pass by a playground and enter the thin growth at the lower corner of the meadow while you are heading to the road post and a shelter. This is the point where you abandon the red mark and turn right onto the path on the forest edge heading to the north. Slightly ascending into an undulated terrain descend later to the Kamenistý potok brook. Cross it and you will walk on its left side. Carry on via rock steps to a wide vertical draining channel and later to a meadow with shelter. This is where the hiking path of the **Kamenistá dolina valley** seasonally closes. Continue through young forest and meadows to the brook. The path runs on the left side of the brook the whole time across the stone avalanches up to the last little island of forest. Now you are entering the dwarf pine forest and the view of the head of the valley opens. On the left side there is the crest of the Kobyla Mt. and majestic Bystrá Mt. (2,248 m). On the right side is the crest of the Grešovo Mt. and the frontier mountain of Veľká Kamenistá (2,127 m). Crossing a fan of little brooks you will ascend on a winding path to the central crest and over wide meadows further to the **Pyšné sedlo saddle** (1,792 m), the third lowest point in the main ridge of the Západné Tatry Mts., which lies on the frontier with Poland. This is where the red-marked ridge tour (0862) starts. Continue westward first in a slightly ascending then steep path over debris and in less than an hour you will reach the top of the **Blyšť Mt.** (2,155 m). The frontier ridge bends northward here. A rather unpleasant stony path leads downward where the red-marked path 2712) coming from Bystrá joins it. You will then descend down a milder slope to the **Bystré sedlo saddle** (1,946 m). The blue-marked path turns off to the Gáborova dolina valley. But you will go around the top of the Banistá Mt. and after a 15 minute walk on red-marked path you will find yourself in the **Gáborovo sedlo saddle** (1937 m) with a deviation of the green mark heading to the Gáborova dolina valley (in case of bad weather or fatigue, you can descend from both saddles to the crossroads Pod Klinom). Ascend from the saddle through the frontier ridge below the northern protuberance of the Sivé veže Mt. and later in a steeply ascending grassy path up to the summit of the **Klin Mt.** (2,173 m). The top will provide you panoramic views of the surrounding landscape. The descent to the **Račkovo sedlo saddle** (1,965 m) is first steep then moderate. The route leaves the main ridge of the Západné Tatry Mts. here and you descend turning left onto the yellow-marked path (8621) fixed by logs to the Račkove plesá lakes (1,717 m). The route leads in dissected terrain to a rock threshold. The paved path around the waterfalls will carry you to the **crossroads Pod Klinom**. Pass by a hut downward crossing the bridge and enter the forest. Continue ahead across the meadow of Prostredná and later on a comfortable wide road to the point where the Jamnícka and Račkova dolina valleys join. The blue-marked road (2711) leads to the **end of the Račkova dolina valley** (890 m).

Pyšné sedlo saddle

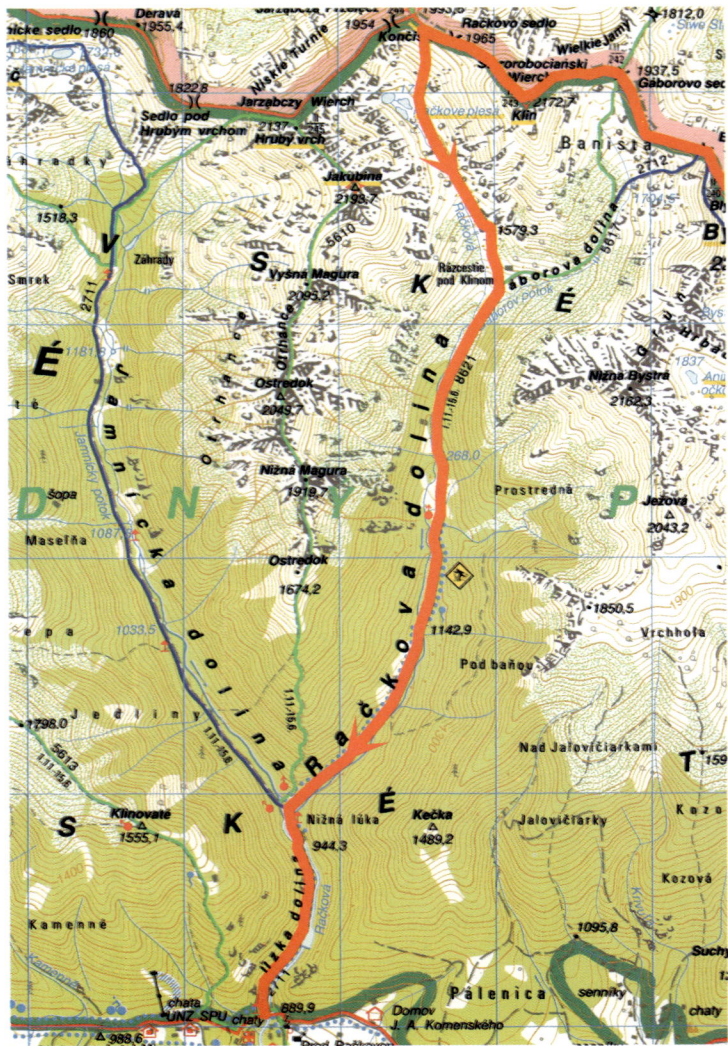

Deravá
*1955.4
Jarząbcza Przełęcz 1953,6
1954
Rackovo sedlo
Końći 1965
*1812,0
Siwe Sl
...cke sedlo 1960
Wielkie Jamy
1822.8
Niskie Turnie
Jarzębczy Wierch
Sedlo pod
Hrubým vrchom
2137
Hrubý vrch
Horobociański
Wierc
1937,5
Gáborovo sed
2172
Klin
B a n i s t
1518.3
Jakubina
2193,7
5610
1579.3
V
Zahrady
S
Vyšná Magura
2095,7
Razcestie
pod Klinom
K
É
B
É
Smrek
2711
1181
oninova
Ostredok
2045,7
Nižná Bystrá
2162,3
1837
Š o p a
1087
Nižná Magura
1919
268,0
Prostredná
P
Jazová
2043,2
Maseľňa
D O L I N Y
N
Ostredok
1674,2
1850,5
Vrchhoľa
1033,5
1142,9
Pod baňou
Nad Jalovčiarkami
*798,0
5613
T
159
J e d l i n y
Nižná lúka
Kečka
É
1489,2
Jalovčiarky
K a z o
Klinovaté
1555,1
S
K
944,3
Kozová
Suchy
Kamenné
1095,8
Pálenica
senníky
chata
UNZ SPU
chaty
689,9
Domov
J. A. Komenského
998,6

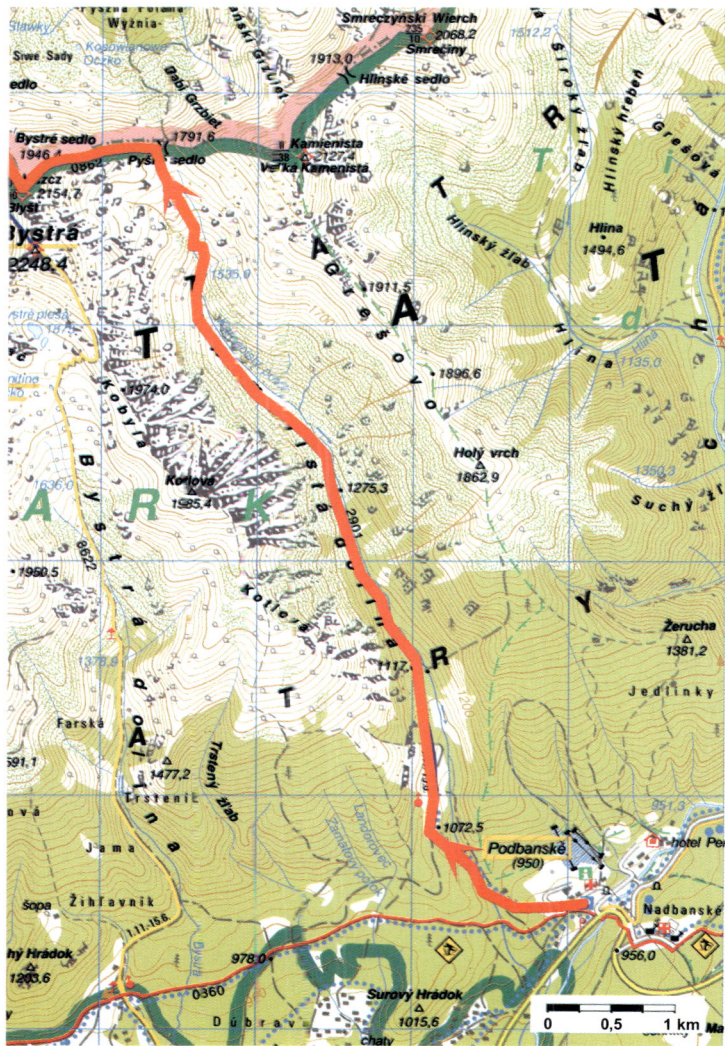

Pyszna Polana
Wyżnia-
Smreczyński Wierch
2068.2
Słowky
Smračiny
Kobylarzowe
Oczko
1913,0
Hlinské sedlo
1512,2
Snve Sady
sedlo
Babi Grzbiet
1791,6
Bystré sedlo
1946
Kamienista
2127,4
Veľka Kamenistá
Pyšné sedlo
Hlinský hrebeň
Grešová
rcz
2154,6
Hlyst
Bystrá
2248,4
Hlinský žľab
Hlina
1494,6
1535,9
1911,5
stré plesá
T
Hlina
1135,0
nting
kO
Kobyla
Agrešovo
1896,6
1974,0
d
ARK
Kurlová
1985,4
Holý vrch
1862,9
1350,3
636,0
1275,3
Suchý ž
Kotlová
2901
A
1950,5
Žerucha
1381,2
Kotlo
R
1378,6
1117
Jedlinky
T
Farská
Trstený žľab
1477,2
951,3
Trsteník
1072,5
na
Podbanské
(950)
hotel Pe
Jama
Žihľavník
Nadbanské
Sopa
1.11.15.8.
hý Hrádok
978,0
956,0
1203,6
0360
Surový Hrádok
1015,6
Dúbrava
chaty

0   0,5   1 km

35

5 The Bystrá Mt.

Hrdovo – Bystrá dolina – Bystrá – Pyšné sedlo – Kamenistá dolina – Podbanské

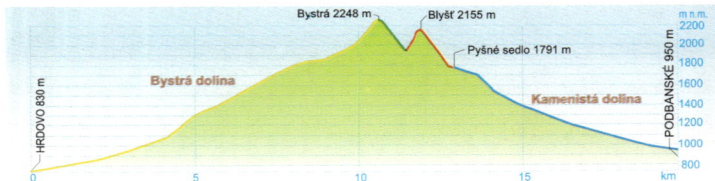

Situation: The Západné Tatry Mts. – South (eastern part).
Starting point: Hrdovo, bus stop, parking lot.
Finishing point: Podbanské, bus stop, parking lot.
Time schedule: Hrdovo – Bystrá dolina 1 ¼ h – Bystré plesá 1 h – Bystrá 1 ¼ h – Bystré sedlo ½ h – Blyšť ¼ h – Pyšné sedlo ½ h – Podbanské 3 h.
Total: 7 ¾ hours.
Elevation gain: 1,418 m.
Map: Západné Tatry - Roháče 1 : 50 000 (sheet 112), VKÚ, š. p., Harmanec.

Grade: Demanding high-mountain tour with high elevation difference and several steep ascents and descents. The summit parts of the Bystrá Mt. and Blyšť Mt. are a bit confusing in bad weather. The paths are closed in winter season.
Basic route: The tour starts at the bust stop near the cottage village **Hrdovo** (830 m). The yellow-marked trail leading through the forest dotted with cottages will bring you to the crossroads with the Tatra main tourist path or *Tatranská magistrála*. After the crossroads the path ascends to the **Bystrá dolina valley**. In the lower part pass by a log shelter good for short break amidst the pleasant smell of the spruce forest. The Bystrá dolina valley is one of the few in the Západné Tatry mountains, which does not reach up to the main ridge. As experts assert, it is less developed than the Račkova dolina valley, its neighbour and its profile is less uniform. The route of ascent crosses several short steep stretches on the valley thresholds. But the Bystrá dolina valley is unusually picturesque due to its smaller dimensions. Before reaching the glacier kettle below the top of the **Bystrá Mt.** (2,248 m) with two lakes called **Bystré plesá** (1,879 m) the meandering path leads to the rocky crest of the **Kobyla Mt.** on the right. Then a comparatively short ascent to the top follows. The return trip follows the blue mark to the **Bystré sedlo saddle** (1,946 m). The path traverses the troughs and the „ribs" of the **Blyšť Mt.** (2,155 m) which is now your immediate aim. You do not have to go to the saddle as some

hundred metres below it your path joins the red-marked trail tracing the main ridge. Choose its right branch. In the **Pyšné sedlo saddle** (1,792 m) which the third lowest depression of the Tatra mountain barrier in the stretch from the Sivý vrch mountain in the Roháče mountains to the Jahňací štít peak in the High Tatras, you will leave the central ridge. To descend take the blue-marked path descending through the whole of the **Kamenistá dolina valley** up to the aim of the trip in **Podbanské** (950 m).

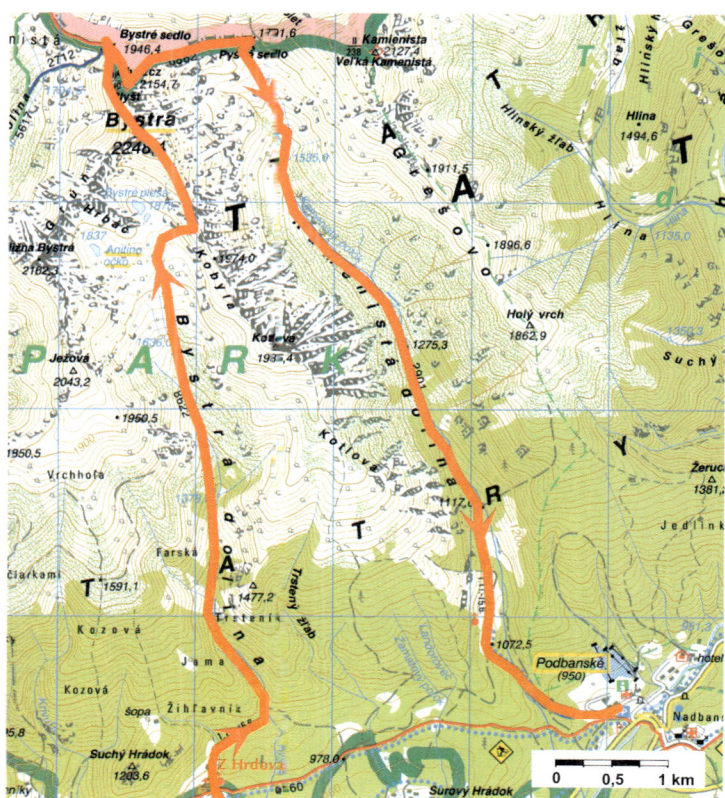

6 The eastern ridge of the Západné Tatry Mts.

Podbanské – Pyšné sedlo – Klin – Račkovo sedlo – Hrubý vrch – Volovec – Jamnícke sedlo – Ostrý Roháč – Plačlivé – Smutné sedlo – Žiarska chata

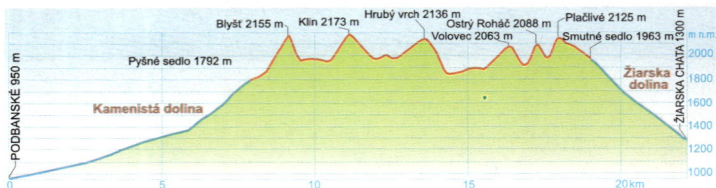

Situation: The Západné Tatry Mts. – South (eastern and central part).

Starting point: Podbanské – recreation village, bus stop, parking lot.

Finishing point: Žiarska chata.

Time schedule: Podbanské – Kamenistá dolina ¼ h – Pyšné sedlo 3 h – Blyšť ¾ h – Bystré sedlo ½ h – Gáborovo sedlo ¼ h – Klin ¾ h – Račkovo sedlo ½ h – Hrubý vrch ¾ h – Volovec 2 ¼ h – Jamnícke sedlo ½ h – Ostrý Roháč ¾ h – Plačlivé 1 h – Smutné sedlo ½ h – Žiarska chata 1 ¼ h.

Total: 13 hours.

Elevation gain: 1,223 m.

Map: Západné Tatry – Roháče 1 : 50 000 (sheet 112), VKÚ, š. p., Harmanec.

In the Smutné sedlo saddle

Žiarska chata cottage

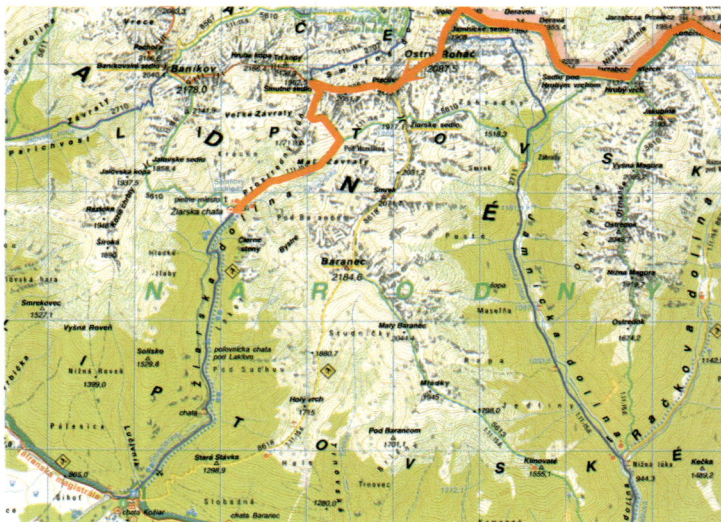

Classification: Extremely demanding, difficult and very long tour with steep ascents and descents. For this trip reliable weather is indispensable and mountain guide should accompany groups.

Basic route: Start at the bus stop of Podbanské and continue up the main road to the turning to **Podbanské** (950 m). The first half of the trip coincides with the route No. 4 which, like this, leads to the Kamenistá dolina valley and then on the blue-marked path up to the **Pyšné sedlo saddle** (1,792 m). Continue on a red-marked ridge route (0862) like in the trip No. 4 westward to the top of the **Blyšť Mt.** (2,155 m), descend to the **Bystré sedlo saddle** (1,946 m) and continue over the Gáborovo sedlo saddle (1,937 m) up to the top of the Klin Mt. (2,173 m). The descent from the Klin coincides with that of route No. 4 up to the Račkovo sedlo saddle (1,965 m). But here, in contrast to the route No. 4, continue slightly ascending to the hardly noticeable tip of the Končistá Mt. (1,994 m) and further to the saddle. Then there is one of the most demanding ascents in the main ridge of the Západné Tatry Mts. on debris switchbacks up to the **Hrubý vrch Mt.** (2,137 m). The route continues by descent on a partially prepared path marked in red and green right downwards. The green mark later turns off towards a trough, you will continue to the Sedlo pod Deravou saddle (1,822 m) and then to the north on a grassy crest up to the Deravá Mt. (1,955 m). The path later turns to the west and a long ascent with the view of the Jamnícke plesá lakes will bring you

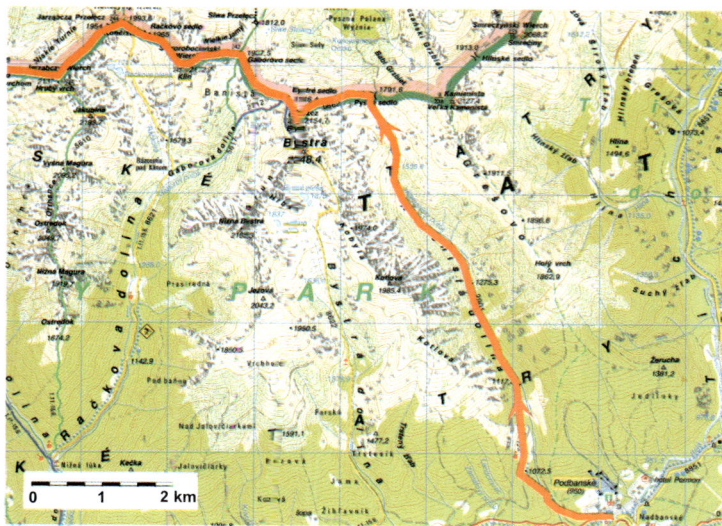

to the round top of the Volovec Mt. (2,063 m). Continue from the top on a wide path leading to the **Jamnícke sedlo saddle** (1,910 m). Continue from the saddle on moderate then steeper ridge to what is called a rock corner with chains used as climbing aid. Passing this physically and mentally demanding stretch you will reach the rock summit of the **Ostrý Roháč Mt.** (2,088 m). Beautiful views of the Roháčska dolina valley with Jakubina and the eastern part of the Západné Tatry in the background are worth the toil. The descent from the Ostrý Roháč Mt. leads westward, among huge stones and down a steep trough secured by chains. Continue on rock steps to an air chimney, which can be climbed down again using the chains as aid. After these demanding stretches there is only a free terrain left before you reach the saddle. Then ascend again a rock path and steps to the wider crest of the **Plačlivé Mt.** (2,125 m), another of the "crown princes" of the Západné Tatry-Roháče Mts. Descend westward over the step-like rock terrain of the Nohavice to the **Smutné sedlo saddle** (1,963 m). Once you leave the saddle behind continue to the left onto the blue-marked path (2707) across the Prostredný grúň up to the **Žiarska chata cottage** (1,300), which puts an end to this demanding trip.

7 A walk on the Tatra main hiking path "magistrála" – the eastern part

Podbanské – end of Bystrá dolina – end of Račkova dolina – Museum of the Liptov Village

Situation: The Západné Tatry Mts.
Starting point: Podbanské – recreation village, bus stop, parking lot.
Finishing point: End of Račkova dolina, car-camping site, bus stop, parking lot.
Time schedule: Podbanské – end of Kamenistá dolina ¼ h – end of Bystrá

dolina 1 ¼ h – end of Račkova dolina 1 h – Museum of the Liptov Village ¾ h.
Total: 3 ¼ hours.
Elevation gain: 185 m.
Map: Západné Tatry – Roháče 1 : 50 000 (sheet 112), VKÚ, š. p., Harmanec.

Classification: A pleasant trip free from steep ascents and descents
Basic route: Start at the bus stop below the Podbanské and continue up on the main road towards the turning to **Podbanské** (950 m). The first short part of the tour coincides with the routes No. 4 or No. 6. It leads on the red-marked Tatra main hiking path (0860) along with the blue mark (2901) slightly to the left and up along the playground on the edge of the forest through the thin growth to the lower corner of meadow towards the road post and a shelter at the **crossroads of the Kamenistá dolina valley**. The blue mark turns right, but you continue straight ahead on the forest road to the west. Turn left after about 300 m on a maintained pathway leading along the contour line. Cross the bridge over the Kamenistý potok brook and continue first straight up the slope and then comfortably slightly descending in forest. Crossing the wide draining channel follow the path through the forest over small brooks and later above the Bystrá brook to a forest road. Continue on the edge of the meadow

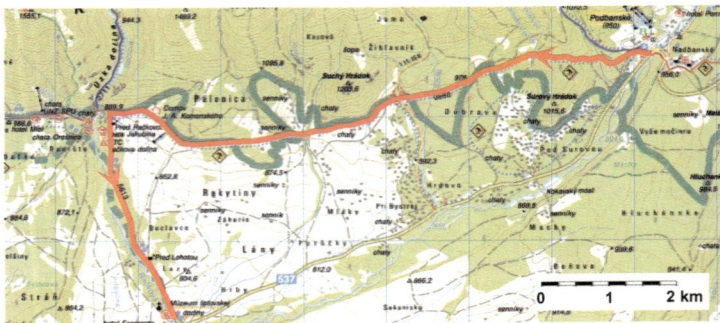

slightly upward and you will reach the crossroads with the yellow-marked footpath leading from Hrdov to Bystrá. If you walk from the road post with shelter up along the meadow edge to a little crest, you will find yourself at the highest point of the trip at the foot of the **Bystrá dolina valley** (1,135 m). The view of wide meadows with numerous cottages opens in front of you. The view of the Liptovská kotlina basin with the whole eastern part of the Nízke Tatry Mts. is also interesting. Now descend taking the path on the forest edge. In the lowest part of the path on

Museum of the Liptov Village

the left is a spring. They you will have to climb to the round ridge of the Suchý hrádok Mt. and passing by a group of cottages you will descend to the Javorníky valley. Pass by a water tower, then crossing little brooks you will enter to thinner forest and continue ascending on the slope of the Pálenica Mt. to a wide clearing with road leading into the wood. The path is steeply descending down over the Rakytický potok brook passing by the Home of J. A. Comenius. The asphalt road will carry you to the crossroads at the foot of the **Račkova dolina valley** (890 m). Turning left you can continue on the green-marked asphalt road (5613) passing by a car camping site and in about 45 minutes you will arrive at the crossroads with the main road as far as the **Museum of the Liptov Village** in Pribylina. The described tour is also suitable for a winter trip on cross country skis because it is easy and safe. The winter trail is normally prepared.

8 The crest of the Otrhance Mts.

End of Račkova dolina – Nižná Magura – Jakubina – Hrubý vrch – Račkovo sedlo – Račkova dolina – end of Račkova dolina

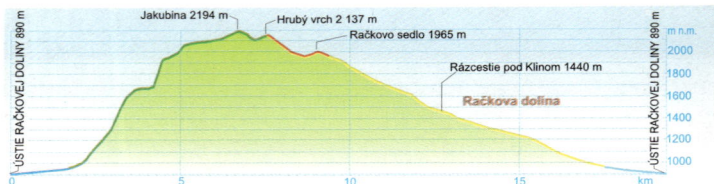

Situation: The Západné Tatry Mts. – South (central part).
Starting and finishing point: End of Račkova dolina, car-camping site, bus stop, parking lot in Pribylina.
Time schedule: End of Račkova dolina – crossroads of Račkova and Jamnícka dolina ½ h – Nižná Magura 2 h – Jakubina 1 h – Hrubý vrch ¼ h – Račkovo sedlo ¾ h – crossroads Pod Klinom ¾ h – crossroads of Račkova a Jamnícka dolina 2 h – end of Račkova dolina ½ h.
Total: 7 ¾ hours.
Elevation gain: 1,304 m.
Map: Západné Tatry – Roháče 1 : 50 000 (sheet 112), VKÚ, š. p., Harmanec.

Classification: Difficult tour in exposed rocks and with great altitude difference. Good weather is the indispensable condition.
Basic route: Start at the **end of the Račkova dolina valley** (890 m) following the blue mark on gravel road (2711) and on the left side of the Račková brook. An ascent through the Úzka dolina valley follows. It heads to the dam and then walking along the brook cross the bridge to the right side and to the crossroads of the **Račkova and Jamnícka dolina valleys.** Turn right onto the green (5610) and yellow (8621) marked path ascending to the Nižná lúka meadow. The hiking marks separate from each other at this place. The yellow-marked path ascends up the Račkova dolina valley. Cross the meadow transversally to the left and into the forest following the green mark and continue on a dug out meandering path up to the upper timber line. It is the most toilsome part of the ascent. Continue walking through the dwarf pine forest and a rock moraine to the first rocky summit of the Ostredok Mt. (1,675 m). Having reached the top pass to a grassy depression and then a steep and demanding crest, which leads to the massif reef of the summit of the **Nižná Magura Mt.** (1,920 m). Continue ascending on a stony path to the second Ostredok Mt. (2,050 m) within the same ridge. You will enjoy wonderful views of the side troughs, in winter constantly threatened by snow avalanches. Now you are walking in a grassy and rocky terrain with varied alpine flora and ascending to the Vyšná Magura Mt. (2,095 m). Then

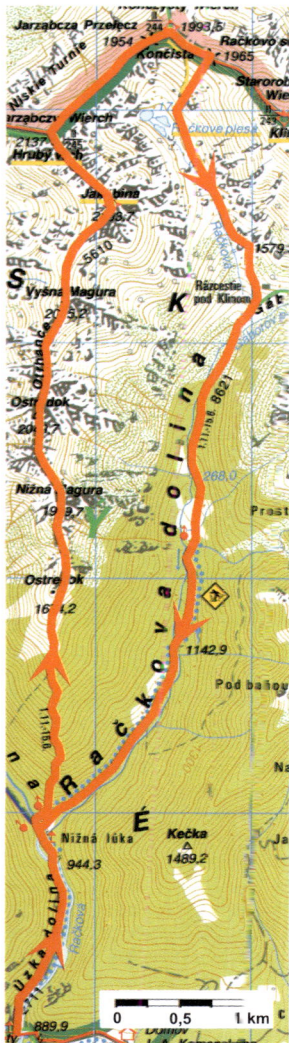

descend to a elongated saddle to ascend again more than 100 meters to **Jakubina** (2,194 m) the second tallest peak of the Západné Tatry Mt. Continue then over a rocky crest to a little saddle and after a short ascent you will find yourself on the **Hrubý vrch Mt.** (2,137 m). Beyond it, on the frontier with Poland you can see the red-marked crest route (0862), the path you continue on to the right and eastward. First there is an abrupt descent on a debris path followed by a less steep stretch over the saddle to Končistá Mt. (1,994 m). The path runs forth mostly on the southern side immediately below the crest as far as to the **Račkovo sedlo saddle** (1,965 m). Your route abandons the main ridge here. Descend turning to the right onto the yellow-marked footpath (8621) fixed with logs which leads to the Račkove plesá lakes (1,717). The path runs in dissected terrain towards a rock threshold and paved footpath around the waterfalls to the **crossroads Pod Klinom**. Pass by a hut, down across the bridge on the left side of the brook and enter the forest. Continue further to the meadow called Prostredná and a wide comfortable road will take you to the crossroads of the Jamnícka and Račkova dolina valleys. The blue-marked road (2711) ends at the **end of the Račkova dolina valley.**

9 The Jakubina Mt.

End of Račkova dolina – Jakubina – Jamnícka dolina – end of Račkova dolina

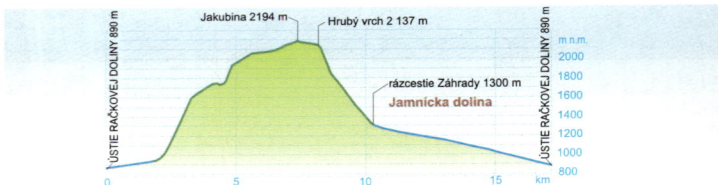

Situation: The Západné Tatry Mts. – South (eastern part)

Starting and finishing point: End of Račkova dolina, bus stop, parking lot.

Time schedule: End of Račkova dolina – crossroads of Račkova and Jamnícka dolina ½ h – Na Prostrednej poľane 1 ½ h – crossroads of Gáborova dolina ¾ h – Račkove plesá ¾ h – Račkovo sedlo ½ h – Končistá ¼ h – Hrubý vrch 1 h – Jakubina ½ h – Hrubý vrch ½ h – crossroads of Jamnícka dolina ½ h – crossroads of Račkova a Jamnícka dolina 2 h – end of Račkova dolina ½ h.

Total: 9 ¼ hours.

Elevation gain: 1,304 m.

Map: Západné Tatry – Roháče 1 : 50 000 (sheet 112), VKÚ, š.p., Harmanec.

Grade: Demanding high-mountain tour with toilsome and steep ascent to the main ridge of the Západné Tatry mountains. Movement on the main ridge and on Jakubina Mt in bad weather requires extra caution, as in mist or at dusk there is the risk of going astray. The paths of this tour are closed in winter season.

Basic route: The trip starts at the **end of the Račkova dolina valley**. Also the next stretch of the route up to the fork of the Račkova and Jamnícka dolina valleys makes use of a comfortable gravel road marked in blue. The yellow-marked stone-surfaced road heads to the Račkova dolina valley. It runs in the forest and on the meadows crossing a mountain torrent several times. You will get some rest at the end of the Gáborova dolina valley. The log building, which the shepherds (1,600 m) formerly used offers protection against adverse weather or in case of emergency you can even overnight there. The yellow-marked route continues to towards the head of the Račkova dolina valley and it is steep in places but the most difficult ascent is close before reaching the summit. Three **Račkove plesá lakes** are becoming apparently ever smaller seen left from the climbing path. The **Račkovo sedlo saddle** (1,965 m) is accessible first by meanders, later by a long steep traverse. Once in the saddle you are not only on the main ridge of the Západné Tatry mountains, but also on the Slovak-Polish frontier. The ridge and

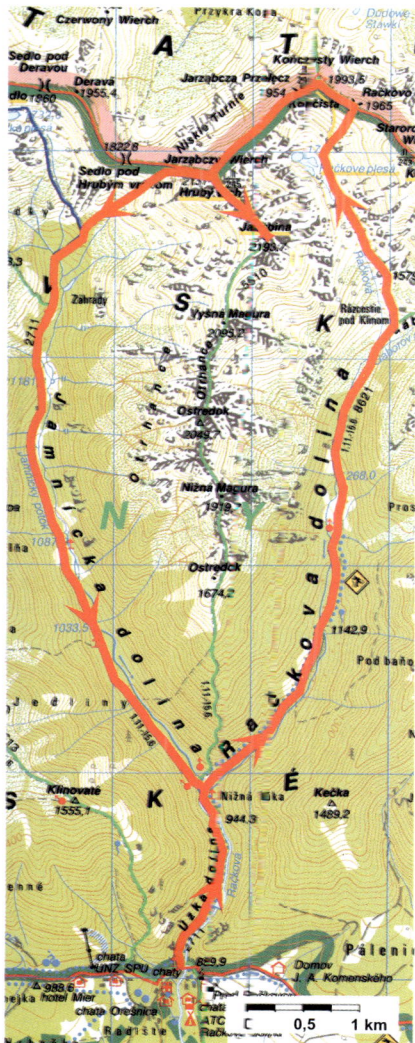

the frontier will accompany you from now on until you reach the **Hrubý vrch Mt.** (2,137 m). Follow the red mark. Beyond the shallow saddle in the south is the **Jakubina Mt.** (2,194 m). This is also one of the important summits of the mountain range providing fine view of the near rocky crest called Otrhance and of the fork of the Jamnicka and Račkova dolina valleys, the same as the more distant landmarks in favourable weather. The basic route returns from Jakubina to the main ridge. To descend to the upper part of the **Jamnícka dolina valley** (1,440 m) use the green marked trail, which crosses in the valley with a blue-marked path coming from the Jamnicke sedlo saddle at the eastern end of the Roháče mountains. The fatigue, result of the difficult tour will perhaps motivate you to decide to cross the long Jamnícka dolina valley rather than to ascend again to the mountain ridge. The blue mark will bring you to the cottages standing at the foothills of the mountains, you have passed by at the beginning of the trip.

10 The Roháče Mts. from Jamnícka dolina

End of Račkova dolina – Jamnícka dolina – Jamnícke sedlo – Ostrý Roháč – Plačlivé – Žiarske sedlo – Jamnícka dolina – end of Račkova dolina

Situation: The Západné Tatry Mts. – South (central part).
Starting and finishing point: End of Račkova dolina, car-camping site, bus stop, parking lot.
Time schedule: End of Račkova dolina – crossroads of Račkova and Jamnícka dolina ½ h – Záhrady 2 ¼ h – Jamnícke sedlo 1 ½ h

– Ostrý Roháč ¾ h – Plačlivé 1 h – Žiarske sedlo ¼ h – Záhrady 1 ½ h – crossroads of Račkova and Jamnícka dolina 1 ¾ h – end of Račkova dolina ½ h.
Total: 10 hours.
Elevation gain: 1,235 m.
Map: Západné Tatry – Roháče 1 : 50 000 (sheet 112), VKÚ, š. p., Harmanec.

Classification: Difficult tour in exposed rocks with artificial climbing aids. Suitable only in good weather. Mountain guide is recommended for groups.
Basic route: Start like in tour No. 8, at the **foot of the Račkova dolina valley** (890) on the blue-marked gravel road (2711) up to the crossroads of the **Račkova and Jamnícka dolina valleys**. Yellow and green marks turn to the right in the direction of the Otrhance Mts. and up the Račkova dolina valley. Your route though, continues to the left. Cross the Jamnícky potok brook and advance on its left side. It is a wide road crossing various torrents flowing from the lateral avalanche slopes of the Baranec Mt. up to a broadened place. Only a narrow rocky road leads from this place over the troughs and brooks of the troughs of Maselná and Pusté. When you reach the hut continue in the forest, then slightly down to a recently forested meadow. The road becomes steeper and it heads up to the meadow **Pod Záhrady** with a shelter and road post. The green-marked path from the Žiarske sedlo saddle comes from the left. Both marks run further in a flat terrain over the brook crossing it to its right side and meandering as high as the upper timber line. The green mark deviates on the crest to the right into the trough below the Hrubý vrch Mt. Continue to the left following the blue mark by a long traverse through the grassy meadow to the threshold in dwarf pine forest and back to the brook. The path proceeds in step-like terrain to a grassy plain to

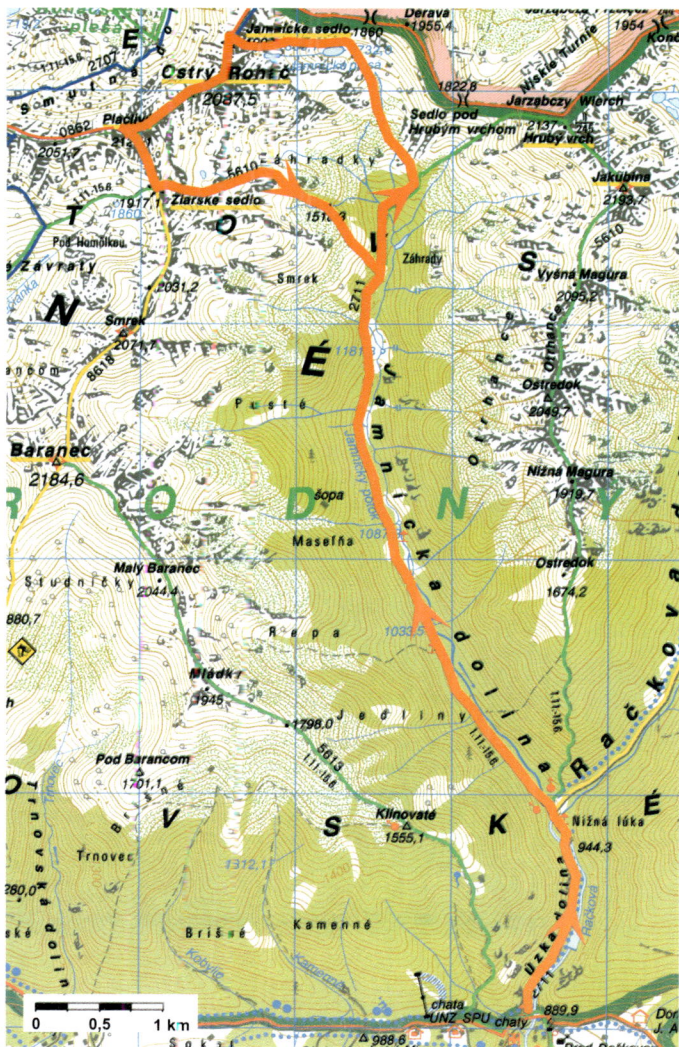

Derava
1955,4
Jarząbcze Przełęcz
1954
Jamnicke sedlo 1860
Ostrý Roháč
2087,5
Plačlivé
1822,8
Niżnie Turnie
Sedlo pod
Hrubým vrchom
Jarząbczy Wierch
2137
Hrubý vrch
0862
2051,7
Záhradky
Jakubina
2193,7
1917,1
Žiarske sedlo
1512,3
Pod Hamžíkou
Záhrady
Vyšná Magura
2095,2
2031,2
Smrek
2711
Smrek
Ostredok
2071,1
2049,
1181,3
Pusté
Nižná Magura
1919,7
Baranec
2184,6
šopa
Maseľňa
Ostredok
1674,2
Malý Baranec
2044,4
Študničky
880,7
Rapa
1033,5
Mlädky
1945
Jedliny
1798,0
Pod Barancom
1701,1
Klinovaté
1555,1
Nižná lúka
944,3
Trnovec
1312,1
Briše
Kamenné
chata
UNZ SPU chaty
889,9
Sokol
988,6

The ridge of the Roháče Mts.

the lower Jamnicke pleso lake. Now you are walking on meandering path around the lake heading towards the **Jamnícke sedlo saddle** (1,910 m). Leaving the saddle turn right onto the red-marked ridge trail (0862) that leads first on moderate then steeper rocky crest to what is called a rock corner. Ascend to a little plateau using the security chain. Pass among the boulders over an exposed rock "horse" secured by chain and you will find yourself on the top reef of the **Ostrý Roháč Mt.** (2,088 m). The reward waiting for you at the top is a wonderful view of the Roháčska dolina valley, the massive mountain of Jakubina and the eastern part of the Západné Tatry Mts. The descent from the Ostrý Roháč leads westward among the boulders down a steep trough secured by chains, by rock steps to an air chimney and down the chimney again with chains. The terrain opens and you will have to cross it before you reach a saddle. Another ascent follows up a stony path and steps leading to the broader ridge of the **Plačlivé Mt.** (2,125 m). After a short rest start southward following the yellow mark (8618) down fairly steep debris path to the **Žiarske sedlo saddle** (1,917 m). Leaving the saddle continue eastward on the green-marked path (5610), first on steep switch-backs down to the little valley of Záhrady and then on a more comfortable path to the dwarf pine forest. Descend over a small brook and on a steep meandering path as far as the **Jamnícka dolina valley**, to the crossroads with the blue mark. Continue down the valley following the familiar route up to the end of the **Račkova dolina valley** or as far as Pribylina.

11 The Baranec Mt. from Račkova dolina

End of Račkova dolina – Baranec – Smrek – Žiarske sedlo – Jamnícka dolina – end of Račkova dolina

Situation: The Západné Tatry Mts. – South (central part).

Starting and finishing point: End of Račkova dolina, car-camping site, bus stop, parking lot.

Time schedule: End of Račkova dolina – Baranec 3 ½ h – Smrek ¾ h – Žiarske sedlo ¾ h – Záhrady 1 ½ h – crossroads of Račkova and Jamnícka dolina 2 h – end of Račkova dolina ½ h.

Total: 9 hours.

Elevation gain: 1,294 m.

Map: Západné Tatry – Roháče 1 : 50 000 (sheet 112), VKÚ, š. p., Harmanec.

Classification: Difficult tour in demanding terrain and great altitude difference. Suitable only in good weather.

Basic route: Start at the **foot of the Račkova dolina valley** (890 m) following the green-marked route (5613) leading from Pribylina. The green mark runs parallel with the main Tatra hiking route marked in red. The green-red-marked path turns left after a while on asphalt road towards the parking lot of the Orešnica cottage. Continue up a stony path to a plateau and then on a meandering path to forest road where the red-marked path turns westward. Now ascend through the forest, crossing a bridge onto a broad road heading to water tower. Continue slightly descending crossing a brook by a log bridge and start to ascend on a dug path up the forest to the Poľana meadow with a hut. The path leads along the left side of the meadow into the forest, which gradually becomes dwarf pine growth. Continue as far as the ridge of the Klinovaté with a great field of dry dwarf pine trees destroyed by fire. The winding path and traverse in the eastern part of the ridge will bring you to the grassy top of the Mládka Mt. (1,945 m). Continue ahead on a rock ridge to a shallow saddle and fairly steep ridge covered by grass and farther to the wide top of the Malý Baranec Mt. (2,044 m), which is often confused with the main summit. The top ridge is left of the saddle; now you ascend the steep, first grassy then rocky, ridge leading to the top. Before reaching it you have to cross a grassy depression and in the conclusion the stony path will carry you to the main summit of the **Baranec Mt.** (2,184 m), which offers fine views of the surrounding landscape. Descend

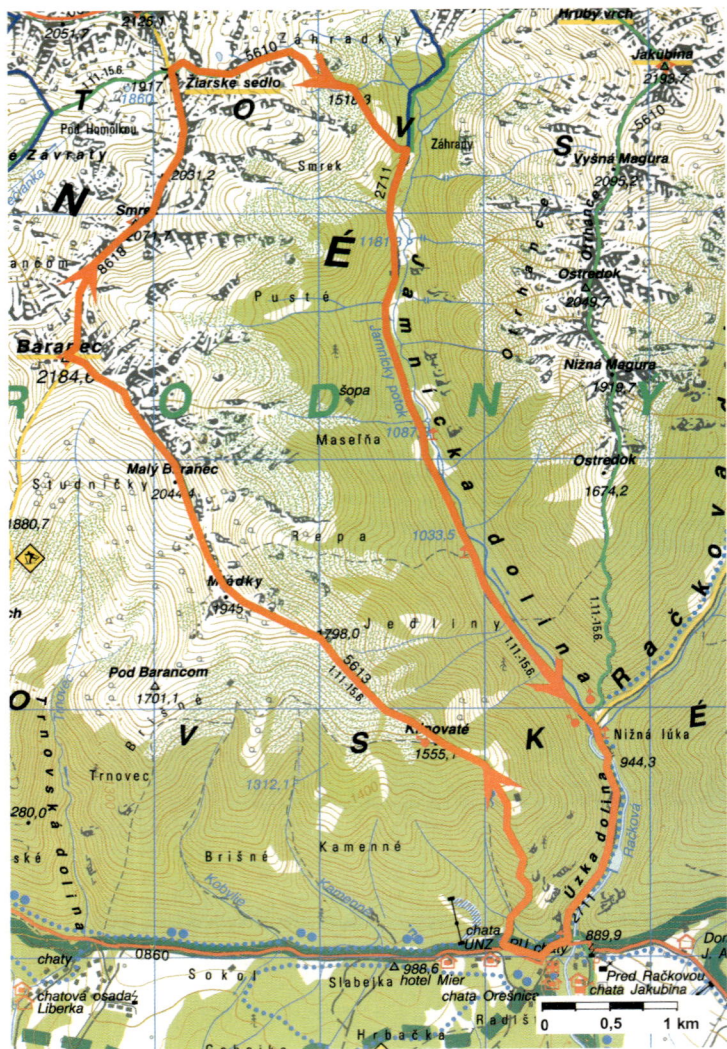

following the yellow mark (8618) to the north on a debris slope to the saddle between the Baranec and Smrek Mts. After reaching the saddle ascend the rocky, in places exposed, ridge across three protuberances advancing to the grassy ridge including the top of the **Smrek Mt.** (2,072 m). Leaving the top descend northward to the **Žiarske sedlo saddle** (1,917 m). Continue eastward on the green-marked path (5610) first on steep switchbacks to the little valley of Záhrady, then on a comfortable path to the dwarf pine belt. The route continues across a little brook, on a steep winding path to the Jamnícka dolina valley and to the crossroads **Záhrady** where it joins the blue mark (2711). Continue down the Jamnícka dolina valley following the blue mark and after about two hours you will reach the **crossroads of the Jamnícka and Račkova dolina valleys**. Reaching it there is only a short walk left to the **end of the Račkova dolina valley** while you can continue as far as the Museum of the Liptov village in Pribylina.

Jamnícka dolina valley

12 A walk on the Tatra main hiking route "magistrála" – the central part

End of Račkova dolina – Sokol – end of Žiarska dolina

Situation: The Západné Tatry Mts. – South (central part).

Starting point: End of Račkova dolina, car-camping site, bus stop, parking lot.

Finishing point: End of Žiarska dolina, bus stop, parking lot.

Time schedule: End of the Račkova dolina – Sokol ¾ h – Hotel Baranec ¾ h – end of Žiarska dolina ½ h.

Total: 2 hours.

Elevation gain: 120 m.

Map: Západné Tatry – Roháče 1 : 50 000 (sheet 112), VKÚ, š. p., Harmanec.

Classification: Easy and comparatively short tour with small altitude difference.

Basic route: Start at the **foot of the Račkova dolina valley** (890 m) choosing the red and green marked path in the direction to the Baranec Mt. Turn left next to the road post near the bridge onto asphalt road to the parking lot of the Orešnica cottage. Leaving the cottage behind the stony road will take you to a plateau where the winding path changes into a forest road. The green-marked path continues up the slope. Your route though, turns to the west along transformer station onto asphalt road leading to the mountain hotel Mier. The route continues now on wide forest road, which slightly ascends to a little crest and then a moderate descent follows. Cross little brooks and arriving at a large meadow with a hut continue beyond it trough the forest to the Kobylie brook. After a moderate descend you will arrive at extensive meadows of the **Sokol** plain with huts and log buildings in its lower part. If the weather is good, you will get wonderful sights of the upper Liptov region and the crests of the Nízke Tatry Mts. Walking on the upper edge of the meadows join a narrow path leading into the forest and this stretch continues as far as the Trnovecký potok brook. In a little valley below the path is a group of cottages, this place is called Liberka. Continue still in the forest and after a while you will find yourself on the turning to mineral

Sokol

spring. Passing by the spring the path leads further to the edge of the forest where on the side crest is the highest point of the route (1,000 m). Forest road will take you to the mountain hotel Baranec and a group of cottages called Horec. This place also offers fine views of the Liptov region. The meadows spreading around the cottages are an ideal ski terrain for beginners. Narrow asphalt road across the brook with the yellow-marked path turning to the right and heading to the Baranec follows. Continue on the road to a sharp bending beyond, which is the aim of our pleasant and comfortable outing – the **end of the Žiarska dolina valley** (880 m). Turn left along the parking lot to the crossroads and towards the house of **Horská služba Západné Tatry – juh** (Mountain Rescue of the Západné Tatry Mts. – South) and the cottage Kožiar. Cross the bridge over the Smrečianka brook and you will get to the bus stop with a shelter and road post.

13 The Baranec Mt. from Žiarska dolina

End of Žiarska dolina – Baranec – end of Žiarska dolina

Situation: The Západné Tatry Mts. – South (eastern part)
Starting and finishing point: End of Žiarska dolina, bus stop, parking lot.
Time schedule: End of Žiarska dolina – Stará stávka 1 ½ h – Baranec 2 h – Smrek ½ h – Žiarske sedlo ½ h – Malé Závraty ½ h – Žiarska chata 1 h – end of Žiarska dolina 1 ¼ h. **Total:** 7 ¼ hours.
Elevation gain: 1,304 m
Map: Západné Tatry - Roháče 1 : 50 000 (sheet 112), VKÚ, š. p., Harmanec.

Grade: A demanding high-mountain tour with steep and difficult ascent to the Baranec Mt. Lowered visibility may cause difficult orientation on the crest in the stretch between the Baranec Mt. and the Žiarske sedlo saddle.
Basic route: Set out on the yellow-marked trial from the **end of the Žiarska dolina valley** (880 m). Asphalt road will bring you to the crossroads. Turn left onto a forest past. The path meandering in a slope cloaked by the spruce forest climbs to the crest of the **Stará stávka** Mt. (1,299 m). The shelter standing at the place where the path surpasses the upper timberline invites to take a rest. The ascent continues through the scree and across the dwarf pine scrub. Higher above the dwarf pines disappear and the landscape changes in alpine meadows, former pastures. A stony path will finally bring you to the summit of the **Baranec Mt.** (2,184 m). The unique view from the third tallest mountain of the Western Carpathians explains why this pyramid-shaped mountain is visible practically from any point of the region. Turning to the north one gets a different view presenting the entire beauty of the Roháče Mts. concentrated around the Baníkov Mt. The Roháče Mts. come closer as you continue in the route on the crest over the **Smrek Mt.** (2,072 m) and as you descend to the **Žiarske sedlo saddle** (1,917 m). If you feel like it, continue on the rocky crest and you can literally touch the rock cone of the Plačlivé Mt. (2,125 m). Basic route drops to the crossroads called **Malé Závraty** where the green-marked path joins the blue-marked one descending from the Smutné sedlo saddle. On the right side of the path there is in the upper part of the **Žiarska dolina valley** the impressively huge **Baníkov Mt.** (2,178 m). The route of ascent to its summit starts next to the Žiarska chata

tourist cottage (1,300 m) over the Jalovské sedlo saddle. It is not part of our trip though. A comfortable paved road will bring you safely to the aim in the **end of the Žiarska dolina valley** (880 m). Turn left along the parking lot to the crossroads and towards the house of **Horská služba Západné Tatry – juh** (Mountain Rescue of the Západné Tatry Mts. – South) and the cottage Kožiar. Cross the bridge over the Smrečianka brook and you will get to the bus stop with a shelter and road post.

14 The Plačlivé Mt.

End of Žiarska dolina – Žiarska chata – Žiarske sedlo – Plačlivé – Smutné sedlo – Žiarska chata – end of Žiarska dolina

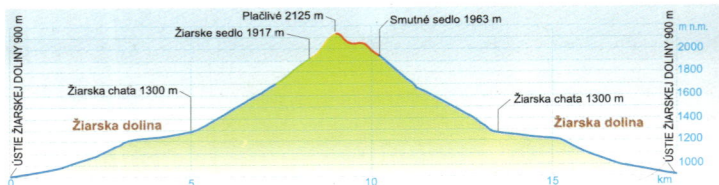

Situation: The Západné Tatry Mts. – South (central part).
Starting and finishing point: End of Žiarska dolina, bus stop, parking lot.
Time schedule: End of Žiarska dolina – Žiarska chata 1 ¼ h – crossroads of Smutné and Žiarske sedlo ¾ h – Žiarske sedlo ½ h – Plačlivé ½ h – Smutné sedlo ½ h – Žiarska chata 1 h – end of Žiarska dolina 1 h.
Total: 5 ½ hours.
Elevation gain: 1,245 m.
Map: Západné Tatry – Roháče 1 : 50 000 (sheet 112), VKÚ, š. p., Harmanec.

Classification: Moderately demanding tour with great altitude difference.
Basic route: Start at the end of the **Žiarska dolina valley** (880 m) from the bus stop following the blue marks (2707). Its first stretch coincides with the red and yellow marks. Crossing the bridge over the Smrečianka brook and walking on asphalt road you will reach the parking lot. Before entering the valley the red and yellow routes heading to the Baranec Mt. diverge to the right. Your route though continues up the Žiarska dolina valley on a firm road. After about 10 minutes you will spot an entrance to a pit on the right side of the road, the evidence of mining activity in the area in the past. Another pit is several tens of meters further on the other side of the brook. The road on the right side of the brook will take you to the bridge and the path, which runs across the forest near the cottages is a shortcut you can take instead of walking the long curve around the meadow. Now you walk on a steep road towards the second bridge along a resting spot where the road gets wider. Continue amidst tall spruce trees towards the double bend of the road below the slopes of the Baranec Mt. The road takes you to a flat stretch before reaching the third bridge over the Smrečianka brook and the bend to the right continuously ascends below avalanche troughs left of the Kozie chrbty Mountains towards the **Žiarska chata cottage** (1,300 m), which offers refreshment and relaxation. Continue along the house of the Mountain Rescue Service to road post where the green-marked footpath (5610) coming from the Jalovecké sedlo saddle joins our trail. Cross the wooden bridge and both marks beyond it run on

a flat crest amidst dwarf pine trees to the foothill of the Prostredný grúň Mt. On your right is a ski lift. Traverse the foothill of the central ridge across the dwarf pine forest as far as the brook with a spring above it. Continue on the side ridge turning left walking in a waterlogged terrain towards the crossroads of the **Smutné and Žiarske sedlo saddles**. Turn right between the boulders and continue on a paved path eastward across a debris field to a terrace and slightly to the left below the steep rock faces of the Nohavice Mt. Marmots can be seen in this place from time to time. Continue above a little basin with the Žiarske pleso lake as far as a little trough. A short bending will carry you to the **Žiarske sedlo saddle** (1,917 m). Enjoy fine view of the Žiarska and Jamnicka dolina valleys before you turn off to the left and upwards following the yellow mark (8618). The route follows a debris footpath and after about half an hour you will find yourself at the highest point of the trip, which is the top of the **Plačlivé Mt.** (2,125 m). If the weather is good you will be able to see the water of both, the Orava and Liptovská Mara dams. A half-an-hour descent over the step-like rock ridge to the west follows. In the final part of the descent down a little bit exposed ridge you will reach the **Smutné sedlo saddle** (1,963 m). Turn right onto the blue-marked footpath (2707) incised into a very steep slope and walk as far as the protuberance of the Prostredný grúň Mt. Continue on the undulating ridge to a little shallow saddle, where you turn left and down and descend on a short switchback to the valley. Paved path running over a little terraces will bring you to the crossroads of the Žiarske sedlo saddle and from then on the route is familiar. It will take you about three quarters of an hour to get to the **Žiarska chata cottage**. Comfortable descent down the Žiarska dolina valley will finish your trip at the bus stop immediately below the **end of the Žiarska dolina valley.**

15 The Tri kopy Mt.

End of Žiarska dolina – Žiarska chata – Jalovecké sedlo – Baníkov – Hrubá kopa – Tri kopy – Smutné sedlo – Žiarska chata – end of Žiarska dolina

Situation: The Západné Tatry Mts. – South (central part).
Starting and finishing point: End of Žiarska dolina, bus stop, parking lot.
Time schedule: End of Žiarska dolina – Žiarska chata 1 ¼ h – Jalovecké sedlo 1 ½ h – Baníkov 1 h – Hrubá kopa 1 h – Smutné sedlo 1 h – Žiarska chata 1 h – end of Žiarska dolina 1 h. **Total:** 7 ¾ hours.
Elevation gain: 1,298 m.
Map: Západné Tatry – Roháče 1 : 50 000 (sheet 112), VKÚ, š. p., Harmanec.

Classification: Demanding and difficult tour with great altitude difference.
Basic route: The initial part of the tour up to the **Žiarska chata cottage** (1,300) coincides with the preceding tour No. 14 to the Plačlivé Mt. After a moderate ascent to the cottage continue by the house of the Mountain Rescue Service to the road post where you turn onto the green-marked path (5610) in the direction of the Jalovecké sedlo saddle. The path passes by the

Memorial to the victims of the mountain accidents in the Západné Tatry Mts.. It traverses the southern slope as far as the brook. Now you ascend on its right side and pass under the **Šarafiov vodopád waterfall** across the brook ascending to the following trough. The winding path ascends in the dwarf pine forest into the wide **Jalovecké sedlo saddle** (1,858 m). Leaving the saddle continue to the right on grassy and rocky crest to Príslop (2,142). Descend to the saddle walking on the steep rock crest. You will have to avoid a part of the indented crest by turning left and then ascend the southern rock top rib as far as to the **Baníkov** (2,178 m), the tallest peak in the main ridge of the Západné Tatry Mts. Now you will have to pass the most difficult part of the ridge. Continue eastward following the red marks (0862). Chains secure exposed terrain. Descend to easier terrain around a rock needle passing through an incision between the

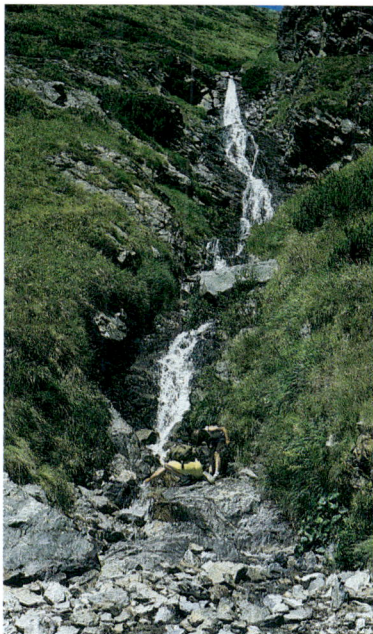

Šarafiový vodopád waterfall

rocks likewise secured by chains. Beyond the grassy saddle is the stretch leading to the second tallest peak of our trip: **Hrubá kopa Mt.** (2,166 m). Have a little rest and then descend to the saddle. Continue passing the exposed **Tri kopy Mt.** (2,136 m) equipped with artificial climbing aids. This demanding pass is recommended only in good weather. Debris path will carry you further to the **Smutné sedlo saddle** (1,963 m). Leaving the saddle behind continue to the right on the blue-marked path (2707), incised deep into a very steep slope as far as the protuberance of the Prostredný grúň Mt. Continue on the undulated crest to a shallow little saddle and then to the left on a short switchback down to the valley. Paved path running across a little terrace will carry you to the crossroads of the Žiarske sedlo saddle and then you will find yourself on a familiar track which leads to the **Žiarska chata cottage** (¾ of an hour). Comfortable descent down the Žiarska dolina valley ends the trip at the bus stop immediately below the **end of the Žiarska dolina valley.**

16 A walk on the Tatra main hiking route "magistrála" – the western part

End of Žiarska dolina – Ľanište – end of Jalovecká dolina – Jalovec

Situation: The Západné Tatry Mts. (south) – western part.
Starting point: End of Žiarska dolina, bus stop, parking lot.
Finishing point: Jalovec, bus stop, parking lot.

Time schedule: End of Žiarska dolina – Ľanište 1 h – end of Jalovecká dolina ½ h – Jalovec ½ h. **Total:** 2 hours.
Elevation gain: 190 m.
Map: Západné Tatry – Roháče 1 : 50 000 (sheet 112), VKÚ, š. p., Harmanec.

Classification: Easy half-day tour in prevailingly descending terrain with nice views.
Basic route: Start at the road post next to the bus stop at the foot of the **Žiarska dolina valley** (880 m) going westward following the red mark (0860) on a wide road skirting the forest. Cross the little brook and slightly ascending you will arrive at a spring in about 20 minutes. Turn off to a hardly noticeable path, which runs first in waterlogged terrain and then in the forest to a grassy crest. Traverse the thin growth to a little saddle where your path joins the same forest road you have abandoned near the spring. Continue across the

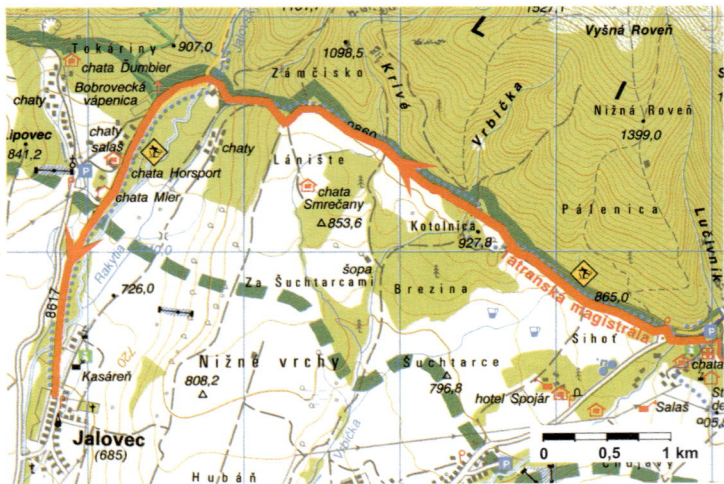

bridge made of concrete tubes over the Vrbička brook and then in the forest to the edge of the meadow. Walking along the tip of the meadow cross the brook and then follows a short stretch through the forest which is becoming thinner. Then you come to a large meadow called **Ľanište**. Continue across the northern protuberance of the meadow to the opposite edge of forest. Walking on its edge you will get on a forest road which steeply descends. After several bends turn right. The route continues again in forest across the Rakytie brook to the edge of a meadow with resting place. Cross the meadow going from its north-western corner to two cottages and continue along them downward, over the Jalovecký potok brook to the road post at the **end of the Jalovecká dolina valley** (800 m). Now you are on the red-marked Tatra main hiking route, which joins here the yellow mark (8617). After about 10 minute walk on the road you will reach the crossroad Na Tokarinách where the red-marked trail ends. Green-marked path (5608) leading to the Babky Mt. in the north-west starts here. You, however, continue to the south following the yellow mark, which now passes among several cottages. Pass through a thin growth along the brook, cross to its left bank and after a while turn left heading to the road post and onto asphalt road. Walking down the road you will get to the bus stop in the village of **Jalovec** (685 m).

The main Tatra hiking path

17 The Baníkov Mt.

End of Jalovecká dolina – Jalovecká dolina – Parichvost – Baníkovské sedlo – Baníkov – Príslop – Jalovecké sedlo – Žiarska chata – end of Žiarska dolina

Situation: The Západné Tatry Mts. – South (western part).

Starting point: End of Jalovecká dolina, parking lot.

Finishing point: End of Žiarska dolina, bus stop, parking lot.

Time schedule: End of Jalovecká dolina – crossroads of Parichvost 1 ¼ h – end of Hlboká dolina ½ h – Baníkovské sedlo 2 h – Baníkov ¼ h – Jalovecké sedlo ¾ h – Žiarska chata 1 h – end of Žiarska dolina 1 h.

Total: 6 ¾ hours.

Elevation gain: 1,378 m.

Map: Západné Tatry – Roháče 1 : 50 000 (sheet 112), VKÚ, š. p., Harmanec.

Classification: Demanding and difficult tour with great altitude difference and occasionally in exposed terrain. Good weather is the indispensable condition for this trip.

Basic route: Arriving at the **end of the Jalovecká dolina valley** from Jalovec following the yellow mark (8617) you will get to the point Na Tokarinách. Follow the yellow mark, which runs parallel to the red-marked "magistrála" (0860). The yellow mark turns left and runs on the left side of the Jalovecký potok brook to the **Jalovecká dolina valley** along the road post at the end of the valley. Cross the lateral tribute of the Jalovecký potok brook and continue on forest road. Now you are ascending the path leading from the valley bottom up the slope on the left. Traversing it you will return to the brook. Crossing several wooden bridges and slightly ascending you will reach a rest place before arriving to a long wooden footbridge at the crossroads of the Bobrovecká dolina and Parichvost valleys. Crossing the bridge you will join the blue (2710) and green (5611) marked footpath leading to the **Parichvost valley**. Crossing more wooden footbridges you will pass to the left side of the valley and ascend for about half an hour in forest up to the deviation of the green mark leading to the Hlboká dolina valley. Continue straight ahead following the blue mark across the little bridge on the left side of the valley and ascend in forest above the brook to the dwarf pine forest. Now you return to the brook. Cross it and ascend on meandering path amidst the dwarf pine forest and rock ribs; continue on a long traverse over a fan of rock troughs on the grassy slope turning to the left to the **Baníkovské sedlo saddle** (2,040 m). Turn right here onto the red-marked ridge route (0862) on a steep, in places exposed ridge, until reaching the top rib, which leads to the highest point of the trip, the **Baníkov Mt.** (2,178 m). After a short rest the return trip starts following the green mark (5610), which leads along the southern rib into a shallow saddle and then you will ascend on exposed rock crest to the second highest point of the trip, the **Príslop Mt.** (2,142 m). Continue southward on a rocky and later wider grassy slope into the wide **Jalovecké sedlo saddle** (1,858). The marking poles will navigate you to the eastern slope with the first islands of dwarf pine trees. The winding path is now descending on the left side of a trough. A traverse to the left into a trough and below the Šarafiový vodopád waterfall follows. Crossing the brook on its left side you will find yourself on a trimmed path, which leads to the piety place of the victims of mountain accidents in the Západné Tatry Mts. founded by the members of the Mountain Rescue Service in 1995. Continue along the house of the Mountain Rescue Service to the **Žiarska chata cottage** (1,300 m) and comfortably descend down the Žiarska dolina valley finishing the trip at the bus stop immediately below the foot of the **Žiarska dolina valley.**

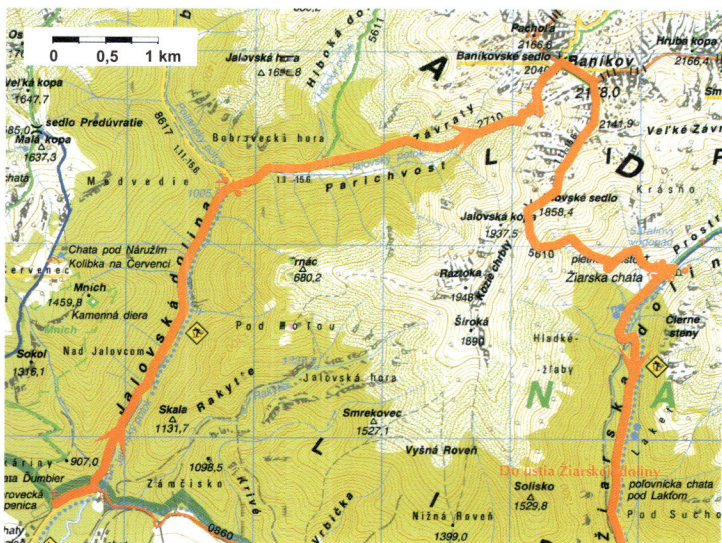

18 The Salatín, Spálená and Pachoľa Mts.

End of Jalovecká dolina – Jalovecká dolina – Hlboká dolina – Salatín – Skriniarky – Spálená – Pachoľa – Baníkovské sedlo – Parichvost – end of Jalovecká dolina

Situation: The Západné Tatry Mts. – South (western part).

Starting and finishing point: End of Jalovecká dolina, parking lot.

Time schedule: End of Jalovecká dolina – crossroads of Parichvost 1 ¼ h – end of Hlboká dolina ½ h – Salatín 2 h – Pachoľa 2 h – Baníkovské sedlo ¼ h – end of Hlboká dolina 2 h – end of Jalovecká dolina 1 ¾ h.

Total: 9 ¾ hours.

Elevation gain: 1,377 m.

Map: Západné Tatry – Roháče 1 : 50 000 (sheet 112), VKÚ, š. p., Harmanec.

Classification: Demanding and very difficult tour for its length, with great altitude difference, the exposed terrain is secured by artificial climbing aids. Suitable only for fit and experienced hikers and in good weather.

Basic route: Start like in the previous trip No. 17 at the crossroads Na Tokarinách at the **end of the Jalovecká dolina valley** (790 m). Your route follows the yellow mark to the **Jalovecká dolina valley** and it coincides with the trip No. 17 as far as the **Parichvost valley.** After a half an hour walk in this valley you will reach the turning of the green mark towards the **Hlboká dolina valley**. Leave the blue mark here and following the green mark you abandon the Parichvost valley. Traverse the little side crests on a forest path until you get to a meadow. Cross it transversally towards a brook. Walking above the brook you are now leaving the forest, which is getting thinner and changes into pine growth while you advance on a well discernible path. A bit above the mouth of the trough below the **Lysec Mt.** (1,830 m) turn left across the main brook. Continue on a winding path on the right side of the trough in fairly steep grassy slope. At this point of the route wonderful views of the glacier kettle below the Spálená Mt. called Vrece opens. Continue as far as the spring and then on the left side of the trough right up (very steep) on little discernible path as far as the side grassy crest, which leads to the main ridge. On the main ridge the red mark (0862) joins your route. Pass through the shallow little saddle to the rock top of the **Salatín Mt.** (2,048 m), which has steep rock faces on both the northern and southern sides. Descend from the top back to the little saddle. Then follows the exposed crest of **Skriniarky** with chains considered one of the most beautiful and most difficult ones to climb in the Západné Tatry Mts. Especially the section above what is called the Zvon (a distinct rock form protruding above the Predná Spálená dolina valley) and that around the Červená skala rock are the most exposed parts of the main ridge. Continue on grassy rock crest and ascend to the top of the **Spálená Mt.** (2,083 m). The path abruptly turns to the south and it is easy to loose way in bad weather at this point. Now you are descending down a less demanding terrain to the saddle and then ascend the rock and grassy top of the **Pachoľa Mt.** (2,167 m), the highest point of your trip. Descend in combined terrain to the **Baníkovské sedlo saddle** (2,040 m) where the green mark (5610) coming from the north ends. Descend down the blue marked path (2710) southward to the **Parichvost valley**. One of the steepest descents in the Západné Tatry Mts. is ahead. The first about 250 m of altitude descend almost directly down to the Jalovecký potok brook. Traverse in the slope of Príslop and the switchbacks in dwarf pine growth will bring you again to the brook. Cross to its right side and then the descent becomes less steep as it runs through the forest as far as the end of the Hlboká dolina valley. Passing the wooden footbridges you will get to the **Jalovecká dolina valley** in about 20 minutes and then in about an hour and quarter to its **end.**

19 The Salatín Mt.

End of Jalovecká dolina – Bobrovecká dolina – Pálenica – Brestová – Salatín – Hlboká dolina – end of Jalovecká dolina

Situation: The Západné Tatry Mts. – South (western part).
Starting and finishing point: End of Jalovecká dolina, parking lot.
Time schedule: End of Jalovecká dolina – Bobrovecká dolina 1 ¼ h – Pálenica 2 h – Brestová ½ h – Salatín ½ h – Jalovecká dolina 2 h – end of Jalovecká dolina 1 ¼ h. **Total:** 7 ½ hours.
Elevation gain: 1,258 m.
Map: Západné Tatry – Roháče 1 : 50 000 (sheet 112), VKÚ, š. p., Harmanec.

Classification: Moderately difficult but demanding tour for its length and great altitude difference with a stretch on the main ridge of the Západné Tatry Mts. Recommendable only in good weather.
Basic route: You can arrive at the foot of **Jalovecká dolina valley** (800 m) from Jalovec following the yellow mark (8617). Start at the Na Tokarinách crossroads on the path parallel to the red-marked "magistrála" (0860). Reaching the road post at the end of the valley turn left and walk to the valley on the left side of the Jalovecký potok brook. Crossing its tributary continue on forest road and afterwards ascend on the path from the bottom of the valley on the left slope. Continue traversing and return to the brook. Cross several wooden footbridges slightly ascending to rest place before reaching a long wooden footbridge and then to the crossroads of the **Bobrovecká dolina and Parichvost valleys** (1,005 m). The blue (2710) and green (5611) marked paths turn to the valley of Parichvost beyond the footbridge. However, you continue on the yellow mark avoiding an island of trees. Turn left across the footbridge in the forest and crossing the side tributaries of the Poliansky potok brook continue as far as the confluence of Podválovec. Turn first to the right then to the left onto a crest and advance in the undulated terrain to a large forest meadow with a hut where an interesting view of the Sivý vrch Mt. opens. Ascend then in thin forest along the Čierne Bobrovecké pleso lake skirted by dwarf pine growths, which turn dry in the summer. After a while you will pass by the Biele Bobrovecké pleso lake. To see it you have to turn right on the path passing a terrain wave. Continue in the forest meadow to its upper end below

a steep slope. There is a sharp left turning and a traverse to the **saddle of Pálenica** (1,573 m) follows. Continue on a path through dwarf pine forest on the red-marked path (0862) through Redikalné (1,651 m) and Pálenica (1,753 m). Now you are ascending eastward on grassy crest over the elevation of Zuberec as far as **Brestová** 1,903 m). Blue mark (2766) coming from the Orava side ends here. Descend to the saddle of Parichvost and continue in fairly steep terrain up the debris crest. The path becomes milder under the top and you are descending to the denuded rocky top of the **Salatín Mt.** (2,048 m), the highest point of your trip. Green mark (5611) coming from the Hlboká dolina valley ends here and it is the route of your descend. Descend first par-

allel to the red mark to a little saddle where you turn left. Later continue abruptly downwards on a hardly discernible path with an interesting view of the glacier basin called Vrece as far as a spring. The following switchbacks will carry you along the brook down to the dwarf-pine growth. Crossing the brook you will walk on its left side on a path, which leads higher above the brook to the first islands of forest. A continuous descent in forest follows as far as the bending above the point where the **Hlboká dolina valley** joins the Parichvost valley. Continue from Parichvost along the blue mark (2710) as far as the **Jalovecká dolina valley**. The familiar stretch marked in yellow (8617) down the valley along the brook to the end of the valley.

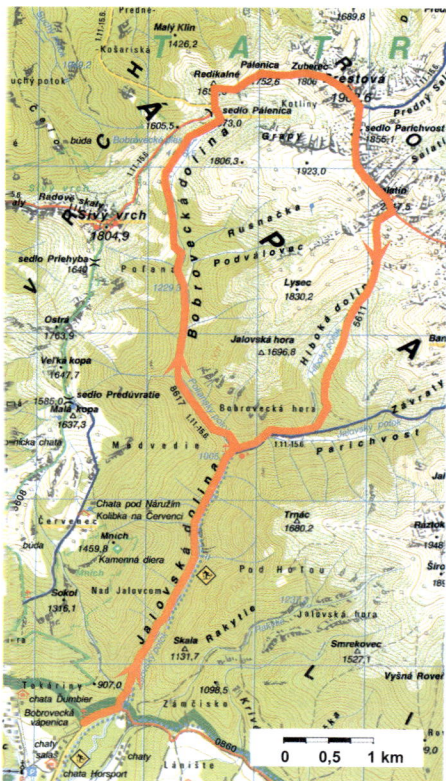

20 The Babky Mt.

Jalovec – Babky – Sivý vrch – Chata pod Náružím – Jalovec

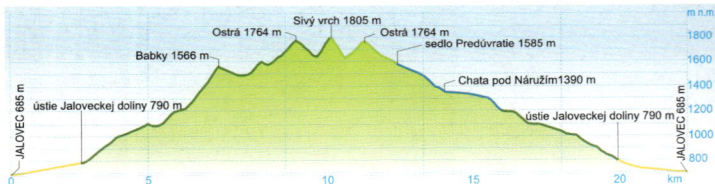

Situation: The Západné Tatry Mts. – South (western part).
Starting and finishing point: Jalovec, bus stop, parking lot.
Time schedule: Jalovec – Tokariny ½ h – Babky 1 ¾ h – Predúvratie ½ h – Sivý vrch 1 h – Predúvratie ¾ h – Chata pod Náružím ¼ h – Tokariny ¾ h – Jalovec ½ h. **Total:** 6 ½ hours.
Elevation gain: 1,120 m.
Map: Západné Tatry – Roháče 1 : 50 000 (sheet 112), VKÚ, š. p., Harmanec.

Classification: Medium difficult but long tour with considerable altitude difference. Recommendable only in good weather.
Basic route: Start at the bus stop in **Jalovec** (685 m) northward, up the street following the yellow marks (8617). At the upper end of the village beyond the last house on the left side is a road post. Turn left onto forest road. After about 50 m the road bends right across small brooks onto the road leading to the edge of the meadows on a little crest. Continue through thin growth behind the recreation buildings and private cottages to a stone road. Cross the brook and you will arrive at the meadow called **Tokariny** with a hiking map and road post. The red "magistrála" (0860) and the green-marked path (5608) start here. Turn over the rampart onto a gravel road and walking in a long bending marked in green you will get to the rocks of the Sokol Mt. The blue mark turns off to the Bobrovecká vápenica and another road heads to the right. Continue on the paved road and the side crests offer you the first views of the valley. Now you leave the forest and enter an open terrain. Narrower road will carry you to a shelter and road post where the blue mark turns off towards the cottage in Červenec. But you enter the narrow valley and ascend the bending road first in the forest and then on steep meadows following the green-marked path passing by a decaying hut to the top of the **Babky Mt**. (1,566 m). The reward comes in form of wonderful views of the environs. Leaving the top of the mountain continue to the north-east on a narrow rocky crest. Later you enter a wide grassy terrain wave and in the western slope you pass by the Malá kopa Mt. arriving

at the **Predúvratie saddle** (1,585 m). The path proceeds on a flat grassy ridge along a spring (may be dry in summer) and among dwarf pine trees around the top of the Veľká kopa Mt. (1,648 m) and the Ostrá Mt. (1,764 m). Traverse the top westward and enter the Priehyba saddle (1,651 m). The debris path also leads to the top of the Ostrá Mt. Leaving the saddle walk first on moderately inclined grassy crest then turn left below the ridge on steep, dangerous when wet, rocky path to the top of the **Sivý vrch Mt.** (1,805 m). On your return trip first descend following your own footsteps as far as the Predúvratie saddle where you turn left onto the blue mark. After passing by the Malá kopa Mt. you will reach a flat grassy crest lying southward and then skirting the left edge of the forest you will arrive at thin growth near the **Chata pod Náružím cottage**, which should be open to visitors from summer 2001. Continue down the footbridge over the brook by a conserved hut. Cross the meadow to the crossroads Pod Babkami. Finish the trip following the green and later yellow marks on a familiar route to **Jalovec**.

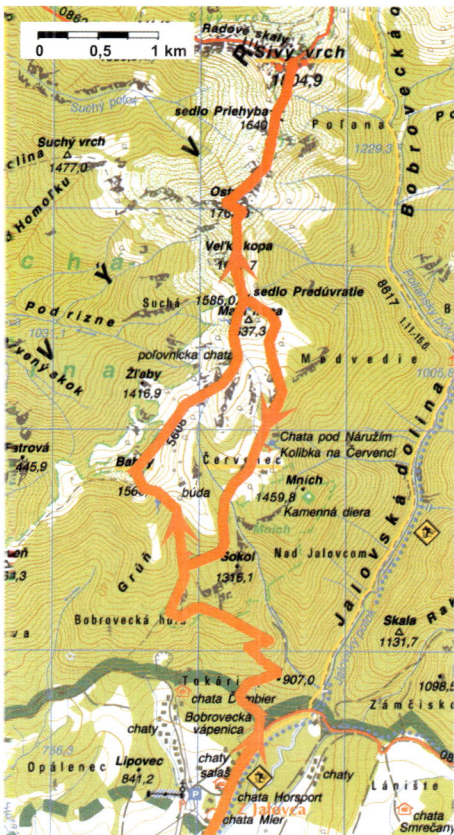

21 The Sivý vrch Mt.

Bobrovecká vápenica – Chata pod Náružím – Predúvratie – Sivý vrch – Pálenica – Bobrovecká dolina – Jalovecká dolina – Bobrovecká vápenica

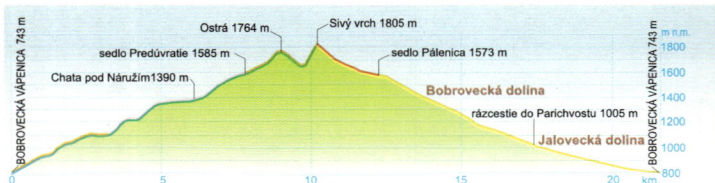

Situation: The Západné Tatry Mts. – South (western part).
Starting and finishing point: Bobrovecká vápenica, parking lot.
Time schedule: Bobrovecká vápenica – Pod Babkami 1 ¼ h – Chata pod Náružím ½ h – Predúvratie ½ h – Sivý vrch 1 h –

Pálenica ½ h – end of Bobrovecká dolina 1 ½ h – Jalovecká dolina 1 ¼ h – Bobrovecká vápenica ½ h.
Total: 7 hours.
Elevation gain: 1,062 m.
Map: Západné Tatry – Roháče 1 : 50 000 (sheet 112), VKÚ, š. p., Harmanec.

Classification: Medium difficult but long tour with great altitude difference. Recommendable only in good weather.
Basic route: Start at the parking lot at **Bobrovecká vápenica** (743 m). The blue-marked route follows the asphalt road to the right at an elevation behind the chapel of the Holy Mother surrounded by the scenes from the Cross Road on wooden pillars. You will arrive at a forest meadow of Lespience and continue upward passing by huts. You will also pass by the Ďumbier Pension into the forest where the route becomes fairly steep and at the top you take the green-marked path (5608). Continue on a wide paved road and the first views of the environs opens as soon as you reach the rocky side crests. Now you are leaving the forest and entering more open landscape and the narrow road will bring you to the **Pod Babkami crossroads.** There is a shelter with road post. Turn right and following the blue-marked path winding in young forest ascend to a large meadow with gamekeeper's hut on your right. Descend traversing along a conserved hut next to the brook, cross the wooden footbridge arriving to the reconstructed **Chata pod Náružím cottage** open the whole year round from summer 2001. Then you pass through a thin growth, continue along the forest edge northward across a grassy crest. Traverse the eastern slope of the Malá kopa Mt. to the **Predúvratie saddle** (1,585 m), The path leads then on a grassy flat ridge along a spring (may be dry in dry weather). The path heads

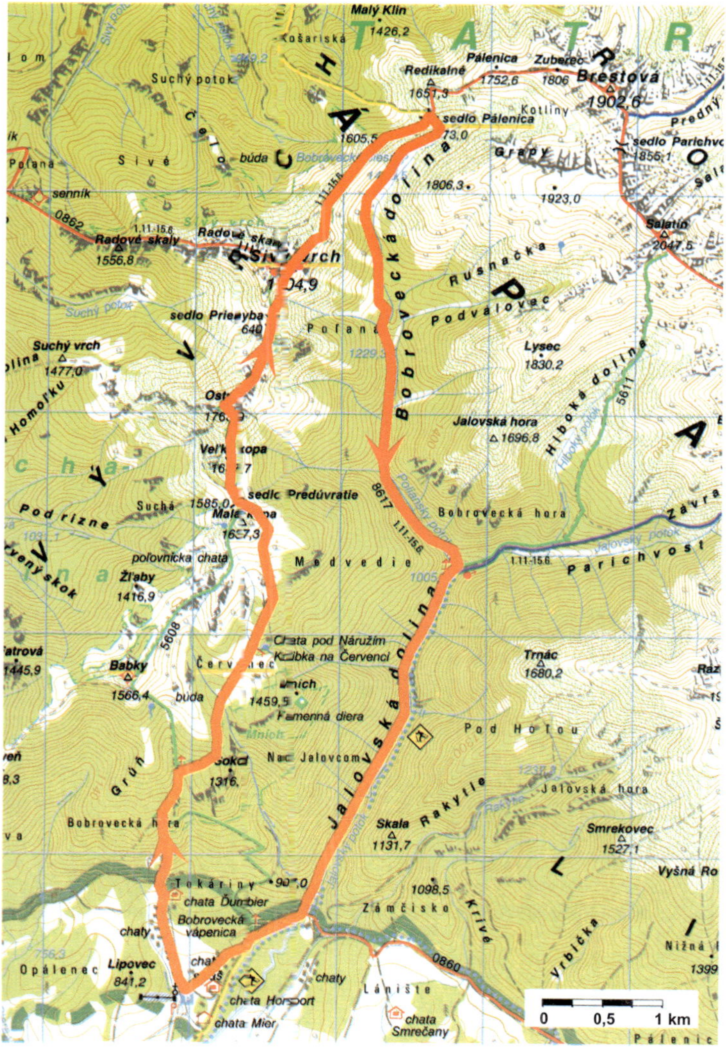

Malý Klin
1426,2
Košariská
Pálenica
1752,6
Zuberec
1806
Brestová
1902,6
Redikalné
1651,3
sedlo Pálenica
Kotliny
sedlo Parichvost
1855,1
Suchý potok
Sivé
búda
Poľana
senník
Grapy
1806,3
1923,0
Salatín
2047,5
Radové skaly
1556,8
Rusnačka
Podválovec
sedlo Prievyba
Poľana
Bobrovecká dolina
Suchý vrch
1477,0
Lysec
1830,2
Jalovská hora
1696,8
Hlboká dolina
Veľká kopa
sedlo Predúvratie
Suchá
Podrizne
Bobrovecká hora
Závrať
Parichvost
Medvedie
polovnícka chata
Žľaby
1416,9
Chata pod Náružím
Kolibka na Červenci
Trnác
1680,2
Babky
1566,4
Červenec
Mnich
1459,5
Kamenná diera
búda
Pod Hoľou
Sokol
1316
Nad Jalovcom
Jalovská dolina
Grúň
Jalovská hora
Bobrovecká hora
Skala
1131,7
Rakytie
Smrekovec
1527,1
Vyšná Ro
Tokáriny
chata Dumbier
1098,5
Zámčisko
Krivé
Bobrovecká vápenica
chaty
Opálenec
Lipovec
841,2
Nižná
Vrbička
chaty
chata Horsport
chata Mier
Lánište
chata Smrečany
0
0,5
1 km
Pálenic

Sivý vrch Mt.

into dwarf pine forest and avoids the tops of the Veľká kopa (1,648 m) and Ostrá (1,764) Mountains. Traverse the western slope of the top of the Malá Ostrá Mt. and enter the Priehyba saddle (1,651 m). The debris path also leads to the top of the Ostrá Mt. Leaving the saddle walk first on moderately inclined grassy crest then turn left below the ridge on steep, dangerous when wet, rocky path to the top of the **Sivý vrch Mt.** (1,805 m). Environs of the Sivý vrch Mt. are charming for its varied rock relief and abundant vegetation. Its is often denoted as one of the most beautiful mountains of Slovakia. Descend following the red-marked trail (0862) north-eastward. The descent is first steep on rocky crest then it runs alternatively through small meadows and dwarf pine growth, crossing the ridge of the Holáň Mt. as far as the **Pálenica saddle** (1,573 m). Turn right here onto the yellow-marked path (8617) and a long switchback will carry out to the **Bobrovecká dolina valley**. If you turn left at the saddle you can follow the yellow mark across the Pribišská dolina valley as far as Zuberec. But our route descends down the Bobrovecká dolina valley along the Bobrovecké plesá lakes. After passing through forest continue on the edge of forest meadow with a hut alternatively on both side of the brook as far as the end of the Parichvost valley. Cross the long wooden foot bridge to the other side of the brook to a shelter and continue down the **Jalovecká dolina valley** as far as its ending. The rest of the trip follows the red mark to the Tokariny meadow and the yellow mark to the Horsport Priemstav cottage. Passing by the cottage turn right on asphalt road and after a while you will reach the parking lot of **Bobrovecká vápenica.**

22 The western ridge of the Západné Tatry Mts.

Pod Bielou skalou – Biela skala – Sivý vrch – Pálenica – Brestová – Salatín – Pachoľa – Baníkov – Tri kopy – Smutné sedlo – Žiarska chata

Situation: The Západné Tatry Mts. – South (western part).

Starting point: Pod Bielou skalou, bus stop, parking lot.

Finishing point: Žiarska chata.

Time schedule: Pod Bielou skalou – Biela skala 1 ½ h – Sivý vrch 1 ½ h – Pálenica ½ h – Brestová 1 h – Salatín ½ h – Pachoľa 2 h – Baníkov ½ h – Tri kopy 1 ½ h – Smutné sedlo ½ h – Žiarska chata 1 h.

Total: 10 ½ hours.

Elevation gain: 1,358 m.

Map: Západné Tatry – Roháče 1 : 50 000 (sheet 112), VKÚ, š. p., Harmanec.

Classification: Demanding and very difficult ridge with numerous exposed stretches secured by artificial climbing aids. The tops are mostly above 2,000 m. Suitable only for fit and experienced hikers and in good weather. Groups and inexperienced hikers should hire a mountain guide.

Basic route: Start at the **gamekeeper's lodge below Biela skala** (820 m). Go back about 100 m on asphalt road northward and turn left onto forest road with information boards and a road post. Following the red marks walk (0862) first on road and later on wide path reaching waterlogged meadows. Continue through the forest which is becoming thinner and you will ascend the crest with limestone massive of the **Biela skala** (1,316 m), the westernmost top of the Západné Tatry Mts. A maintained path leads further along the ridge, and you should enjoy wonderful and unique views of the valley of the Orava and Váh rivers, and practically the whole of the regions of Orava and Liptov. Walking through the dwarf pine growth you will gradually reach the "rock town" of the Radové skaly rocks. Continue ascending across the stretches secured by artificial climbing aids as far as the distinct rock top of the **Sivý vrch Mt.** (1,805 m) with fine view of the environs and if it is in springtime, also with beautiful flora. Green mark (5608) coming from the Babky Mt. joins your route at this point. Now descend the rocky crest (unpleasant in wet weather) onto the beaten path overgrown by roots of dwarf pine trees, which leads to the **saddle of Pálenica** (1,573 m). The yellow marked path (8617) coming from the

Bobrovecká dolina valley joins your path. Continue on the path across the
dwarf pine forest to Redikalné and Pálenica (1,753 m) and further on grassy
crest passing the Zuberec elevation point to the **Brestová Mt.** (1,903 m). Blue
mark (2766) comes there from the region of Orava. You, however, descend to
the saddle of Parichvost and continue on a steep debris crest. The path
becomes easier and then you ascend to the top of the **Salatín Mt.** (2,048). The
green mark (5611) coming from the Hlboká dolina valley ends here. After the
descent from the top there is the exposed crest of Skriniarky secured by
chains, and the grassy, in places rocky, crest leading to the top of the **Spálená
Mt.** (2,083 m). The path suddenly changes its direction southward and now
you descend in easier terrain to a little saddle. A short steep ascent to the top
of the **Pachoľa Mt.** (2,167 m) follows. Descend to the **Baníkovské sedlo saddle** (2,054 m) where the blue (2710) mark coming from the south and green
(5610) mark coming from the north, end. The ascent from the saddle is steep
and it runs on a dissected ridge. The reward is matching, you have just
climbed the most attractive summit of the mountain range, the tallest peak in
the main ridge of the Západné Tatry Mts., **Baníkov Mt.** (2,178 m). Also the

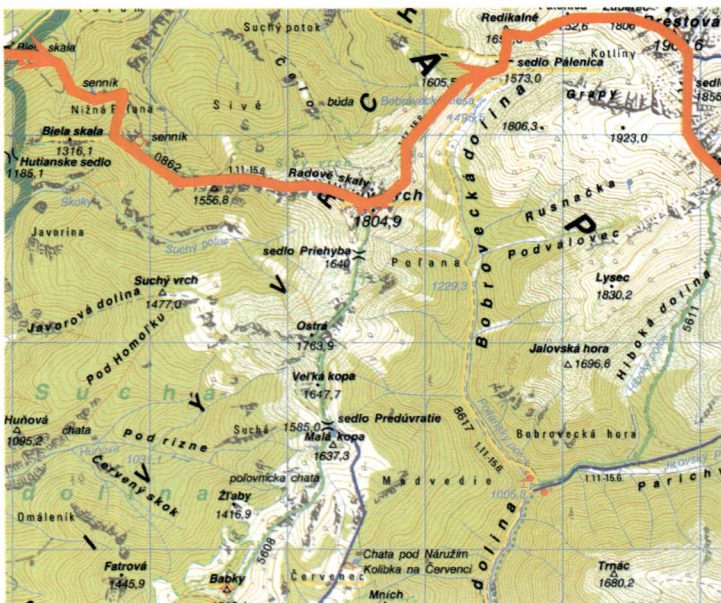

green mark coming from the Jalovecké sedlo saddle ends at the top. But the most difficult part of the ridge is still ahead. Continue eastward where chains (very risky in wet or freezing weather) secure the exposed parts of the terrain. Cross the incision in rock and descend to easier terrain around the rock needle using the artificial climbing aids available. Beyond the wide meadow saddle the ascent to the **Hrubá kopa Mt.** (2,166 m) follows. Descend from the top to a saddle. A passage through exposed terrain of **Tri kopy Mt.** (2,136 m), a three-top bulky rock form, secured by chains follows. This technically demanding passage is recommendable only in good weather. Having passed the third top descend on a debris path to the **Smutné sedlo saddle** (1,963 m). Leaving the saddle behind turn right onto the blue-marked path (2707) incised in very steep slope and follow it as far as the side crest of the Prostredný grúň Mt. Continue on the meandering crest as far as a shallow little saddle and then to the left down to a little valley. Paved path leading across a little terrace will carry you to the crossroads at the Žiarske sedlo saddle and further on familiar route to the **Žiarska chata cottage** (1,300 m). We recommend booking the accommodation in advance as you will be very tired when you get there.

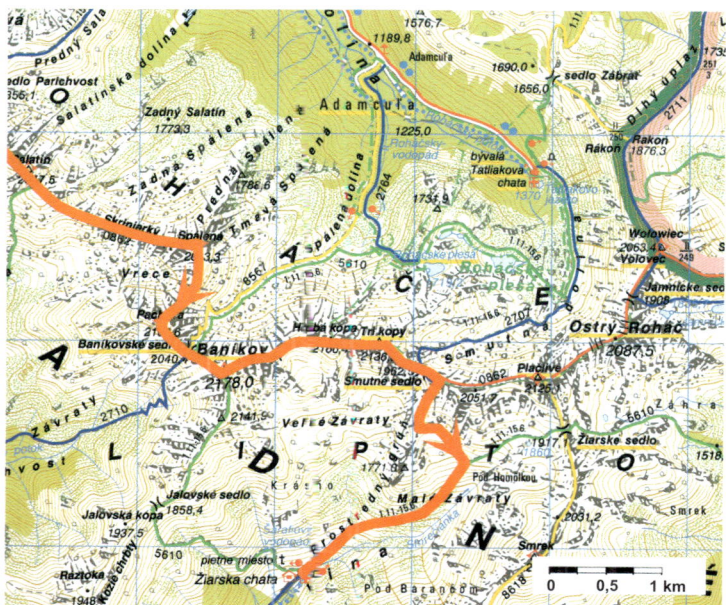

23 Over the ridge of the Západné Tatry Mts.

Žiarska chata – Žiarske sedlo – Plačlivé – Ostrý Roháč – Volovec – Roháčska dolina – Chata Zverovka

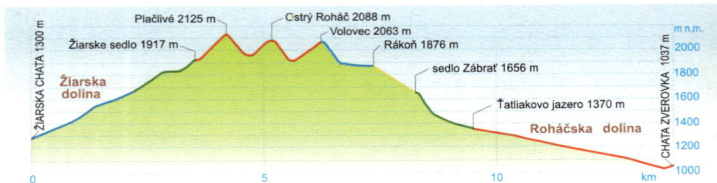

Situation: The Západné Tatry Mts. – South (central part).
Starting point: Žiarska chata.
Finishing point: Chata Zverovka, bus stop, parking lot.
Time schedule: Žiarska chata – crossroads of Smutné and Žiarske sedlo ¾ h –

Žiarske sedlo ½ h – Plačlivé ½ h – Ostrý Roháč 1 h – Volovec ¾ h – Roháčska dolina 1 ¼ h – Chata Zverovka 1 ½ h.
Total: 6 ¼ hours.
Elevation gain: 1,088 m.
Map: Západné Tatry – Roháče 1 : 50 000 (sheet 112), VKÚ, š. p., Harmanec.

Classification: Demanding and comparatively long and exposed tour with great altitude difference.
Basic route: Start at the **Žiarska chata cottage** (1,300 m) on blue-marked path running by the house of Horská služba (Mountain Rescue Service) to the road post where the green-marked path (5610) coming from the Jalovecké sedlo saddle joins our route. Both marks continue further over the wooden footbridge on flat crest in dwarf pine forest as far as the foothill of the Prostredný grúň Mt. The ascent is not very demanding and you can admire the wonderful silhouette of the surrounding peaks, especially the Baranec Mt. The ski lift on your right enhances the attractiveness of the place. Now you are traversing the flank of the central crest and heading to the little brook with a spring above it. The traverse leads on lateral crest to the left up through waterlogged terrain and finally reaches the **crossroads of the Smutné and Žiarske sedlo saddles**. Turn right and continue slightly to the left below the steep rock faces of the Nohavice. This place is a favourite one of the Tatra marmots. Continue above a little basin with the Žiarska Pleso Lake as far as a little trough and then ascend to the **Žiarske sedlo saddle** (1,917 m). Enjoy the views of the Žiarska and Jamnicka dolina valleys and turn left ascending the steep slope following the yellow marks (8618). The route leads in places on debris path and after about half an hour you will find yourself at the highest point of the tour at the top of the **Plačlivé Mt.** (2,125 m) with

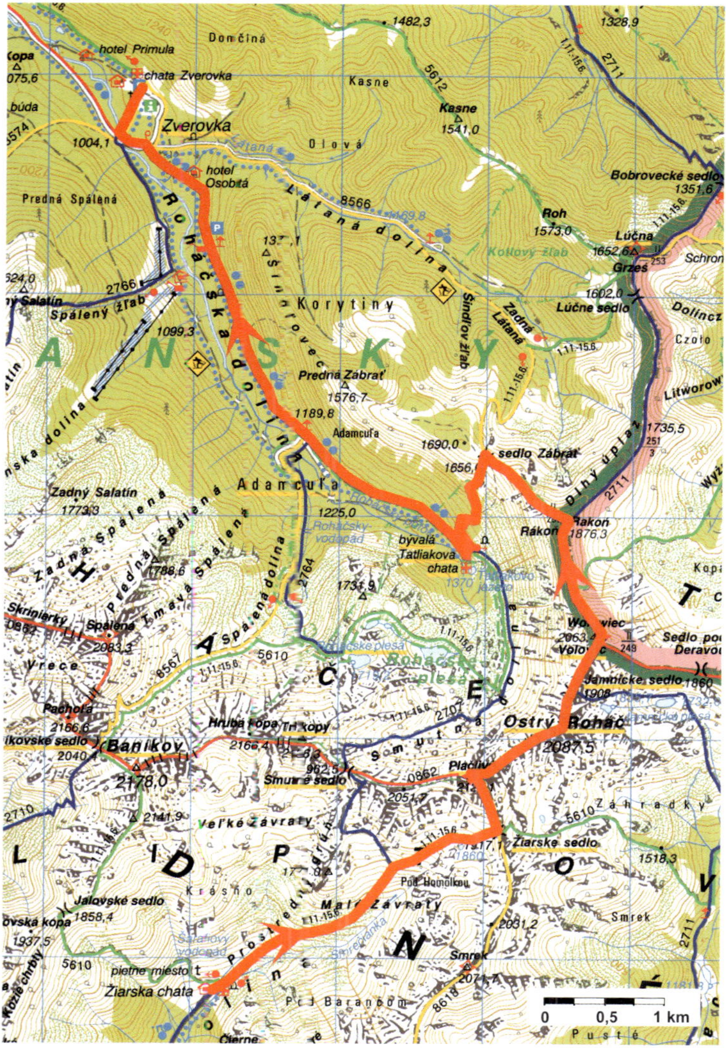

Žiarske pleso lake

unique views of the Smutná dolina valley. Have a short rest and then descend following the red-marked crest (0862) over the step-like rock crest eastward to the saddle. A short ascent on a crest leading to what is called a rocky corner follows. Using the chains ascend the double top of the **Ostrý Roháč Mt.** (2,088 m). The reef of the Ostrý Roháč is the favourite destination of the visitors of the Západné Tatry Mts. Descend over the rocky blocks across the sharp crest secured by chain down the step-like rib to a steep corner and farther on an easier path leading to the **Jamnícke sedlo saddle** (1,910 m). The blue marked path joins your route here. Your trail leads on a gradually ascending path as far as the **peak of Volovec** (2,063 m) standing on the Slovak-Polish frontier. After having admired the open views of both the Slovak and Polish sides of the Tatras leave the red-marked ridge route and follow the blue mark (2711), which coincides with the frontier. Turn left onto the yellow marked path (8566) heading to Zadná Zábrať, which ends at the Zábrať saddle (1,656 m). Continue from the saddle on the green mark (5610) and descend on the winding path in steep slope to the Ťatliakovo jazero lake. Passing comfortably through the Roháčska dolina valley on asphalt road you will arrive at the **Chata Zverovka cottage** (1,037 m).

24 The Osobitá Mt.

Chata Zverovka – Sedlo pod Osobitou – Lúčna – Látaná dolina – Chata Zverovka

Situation: The Západné Tatry Mts. – North (eastern part).

Starting and finishing point: Chata Zverovka, bus stop, parking lot.

Time schedule: Chata Zverovka - Hotel Primula ¼ h – Sedlo pod Osobitou 1 ¾ h

– Lúčna 2 h – Látaná dolina 1 h – Chata Zverovka 1 ¼ h.

Total: 6 ¼ hours.

Elevation gain: 616 m.

Map: Západné Tatry – Roháče 1 : 50 000 (sheet 112), VKÚ, š. p., Harmanec.

Classification: Medium difficult, comparatively comfortable trip with interesting views.

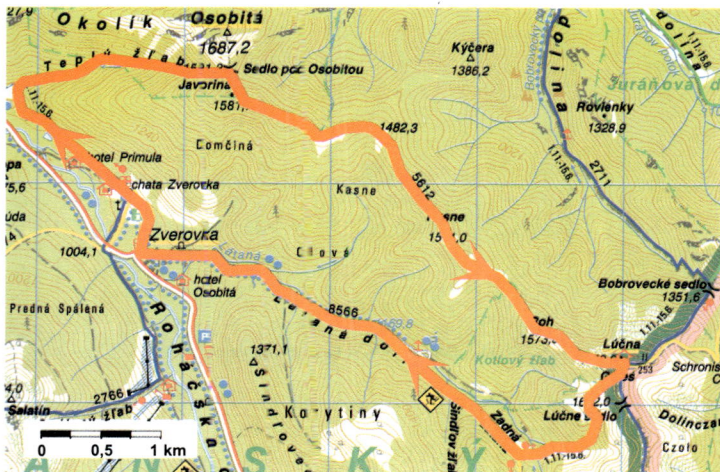

Basic route: The trip starts at the road post near the **Chata Zverovka cottage** (1,037 m). Follow the green marks (5612) along the house of Horská služba (Mountain Rescue Service) of Západné Tatry Mts. – north and continue in the forest on comfortable path along the **Primula hotel**. The road leads along the lake through the forest to the Pučatina meadow. Walk across the meadow north-eastward on the edge of forest until you reach the entering part of the Javorina valley. Turn right to the part called Teplý žľab trough and continue along the brook up the maintained path. On the opposite side of this little valley is an avalanche trough with young growth in its lower part. Traverse the trough, enter the forest and cross it using a rocky path advancing to the spot, where the forest suddenly ends. Continue on an evidently much used path to the grassy **Sedlo pod Osobitou saddle** (1,550 m). Abundant representatives of the alpine flora growing at this place will certainly attract your attention. The yellow mark leading to the Osobitá Mt. (1,687 m) is closed because of nature conservation reasons. The whole area is now nature reserve. Continue from the saddle slightly upwards to the elevation point of Javorina (1,581 m). Now you walk in dwarf pine forest to the crest of Domčiná, enter into a thin forest and then descend on a grassy crest to the **Kasne** meadow with

The ridge of the Západné Tatry Mts.

wonderful view of the Roháče Mts. Continue down the ridge, in places muddy, over a shallow little saddle and ascend again in a thin forest going around the top of the Roh Mt. (1,573 m). Descend a bit through the dwarf pine forest to the little saddle and ascend again to the frontier with the **Na Lúčnej cross-roads** (1,653 m) The blue-marked path (2711), which passes on the frontier ridge from Rákoň (1,876 m) to the Bobrovecké sedlo saddle (1,352 m) joins our route here. Walking on a wide ridge turn off the frontier to a trough and descend down its edge to a traverse and cross the brook. Later advance down the young forest heading to the meadow in the Zadná Látaná dolina valley. The green mark ends at the **Látaná dolina crossroads**. Continue on the yellow-marked path, which leads from the Zábrať saddle (1,656 m). Descend down the young forest, later the path becomes steeper and when you reach the edge of a little meadow, continue to the right crossing the footbridge over the brook to asphalt road. Comfortably walking down the valley you pass by the Partisan Cemetery and walk as far as the turning to the **Chata Zverovka cottage**. Those who are not accommodated at the cottage of Zverovka or in its immediate environs will continue on the red-marked road across the meadow of Brestová, with the Museum of the Orava Village as far as **Zuberec** (734 m).

The alpine meadow of Zverovka

25 The Ostrý Roháč and Plačlivé Mts.

Chata Zverovka – Ostrý Roháč – Plačlivé – Smutné sedlo – Roháčske plesá – Chata Zverovka

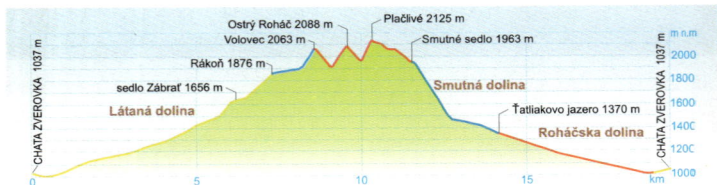

Situation: The Západné Tatry Mts. – North (eastern part).

Starting and finishing point: Chata Zverovka, bus stop, parking lot.

Time schedule: Chata Zverovka – crossroads of Zadná Látaná dolina 1 ¼ h – Zábrať ¾ h – Rákoň ½ h – Volovec ¾ h – Jamnícke sedlo ¼ h – Ostrý Roháč ¾ h – Plačlivé ¼ h – Smutné sedlo ½ h – crossroads of Smutná dolina 1 h – Roháčsky vodopád 1 ½ h – Adamcuľa ½ h – Chata Zverovka ¾ h.

Total: 8 ¾ hours.

Elevation gain: 1,088 m.

Map: Západné Tatry – Roháče 1 : 50 000 (sheet 112), VKÚ, š. p., Harmanec.

Grade: Very demanding high-mountain tour with big elevation gain. Exposed stretches are provided by artificial technical aids. Not recommended in adverse weather conditions. Most of its parts are closed in winter time.

Basic route: Start below the **Chata Zverovka cottage** (1,037 m) going south-east. The yellow-marked asphalt road heads to the Látaná dolina valley. Before reaching its upper end, abandon the road. Cross the footbridge over the brook and enter spruce forest. At the crossroads at the upper end of the meadow in the Zadná Látaná dolina stay on the yellow-marked trail which ends in the wide grassy **Zábrať saddle** (1,656 m). Ascending to the saddle you finally find yourself at an alpine or high-mountain level. From now on you will move among scree, rocks and dwarf pine scrub until the evening. The path ascends from the saddle to the first top of the route the **Rákoň Mt.** (1,876 m) standing on the Polish-Slovak state border. After a short descent to a shallow saddle ascend again to the neighbouring mountain of **Volovec** (2,063 m). This is the first one of the three two thousand metre tall mountains with panoramic views considered the most beautiful in the whole mountain range of Západné Tatry. Once on the top of the Volovec Mt. you leave the state border and descend to the Jamnícke sedlo saddle (1,908 m). The most difficult stretch of the tour follows. You have to proceed on a narrow and highly exposed crest ascending to the **Ostrý Roháč Mt.** (2,088 m) secured with chains. Even while you are descending you will have

Teplý žľab
1687,2
Sedlo pod Osobitou
1521,3
Javorina
1581,2
Kýčera
1386,2
Domčiná
1482,3
Rovienky
1328,9
hotel Primula
chata Zverovka
Kasne
opa
75,6
búda
574
Zverovka
1004,1
Olevá
Kasne
1541,0
Bobrovecké sedlo
1351,6
hotel
Osobitá
Látaná dolina
8566
469,8
Roh
1573,0
Lúčna
1652,6
Grześ
Schroni
Predná Spálená
Roháčska dolina
Šindľovec
1371,1
Korytiny
Kollový žľab
Lúčne sedlo
1602,0
Czoło
Dolinczy
24,0
2766
Spálený žľab
1099,3
Predná Zabrať
1576,7
1189,8
Smutný žľab
Zadná
Dlhý úplaz
2711
1735,5
251
3
Litworowy
A   N   S   K   Y
Adamcuľa
Adamcuľa
1225,0
Roháčsky
vodopád
1690,0
1656,0
sedlo Zábrať
Rákoň
1876,3
Kopa
Zadný Salatín
1773,3
bývalá
Tatliakova
chata
1970
Rákoň
Zadná Spálená
Predná Spálená
1788,6
Tmavá Spálená
2764
1731,9
Spálená dolina
Volovec
2063,9
Sedlo pod
Deravou
Skriniarky
Spálená
2083,3
8567
5610
Roháčske plesá
Jamnické sedlo
1860
1908
Vrece
Pachoľa
2166,6
Hrubá kôpa
Tri kopy
2166,4
Ostrý Roháč
2087,5
kovské sedlo
2040,
Baníkov
2178,0
962,6
Smutná
Smutné sedlo
Smutná dolina
Placlivô
2125,
2051,4
Žiarske sedlo
1518,3
2141,9
Veľké Závraty
1917,1
Záhradky
5610
L   I   D
P   T   O
V
Jalovské sedlo
1858,4
Kráshô
Prič Homôlkou
1860
Malé Závraty
2081
Smrek
ská kopa
1937,5
N
0   0,5   1 km

85

Roháče Mts.

to use your hands and aids fixed in the rock. The next stretch beyond the saddle between the two twin mountains is a little bit easier. It leads in the scree and on a rocky path to the **Plačlivé Mt.** (2,125 m). Then follows the descent to the Smutné sedlo saddle (1,963 m). Seen from the deep depression in the main ridge this inseparable couple of mountains is most beautiful. For the descent to the **Smutná dolina valley** take the blue-marked trail and half-way to Ťatliakovo jazero lake turn left to the green trail. It is an easy walk afterwards, which will bring you to the charming Roháčske plesá lakes lying in a deep glacier basin filled with scree and moraines. First go round Prvé Roháčske pleso lake (1,563 m), which is the largest of the four lakes. From the highest situated high-mountain lake Štvrté Roháčske pleso (1,718 m) the trail descends via the blue-marked path down the **Spálená dolina valley**. Beyond the rocky threshold it joins the yellow trail. In the lower part is a good stopping-off point to see the **Roháčsky vodopád waterfall** (1,300 m) the tallest in the Západné Tatry Mts. After passing Adamcuľa (1,180 m) the route changes. The forest path becomes an asphalt road ending at the aim, the **Chata Zverovka cottage** (1,037 m).

26 The Hrubá kopa and Baníkov Mts.

Chata Zverovka – Ťatliakovo jazero – Smutné sedlo – Baníkov – Roháčsky vodopád – Chata Zverovka

Situation: The Západné Tatry Mts. – North (eastern part)
Starting and finishing point: Chata Zverovka, bus stop, parking lot.
Time schedule: Chata Zverovka – Ťatliakovo jazero 1 ¼ h – Smutné sedlo 2 h – Tri kopy ½ h – Banikov 2 h – Baníkovské sedlo ¼ h – Roháčsky vodopád 2 h – Chata Zverovka 1 ¼ h. **Total:** 9 ¼ hours.
Elevation gain: 1,141 m.
Map: Západné Tatry – Roháče 1 : 50 000 (sheet 112), VKÚ, š. p., Harmanec.

Grade: Very demanding high-mountain tour. Exposed stretches on the main mountain ridge are secured with artificial technical aids. Not recommended in winter season.

Basic route: The initial section of the tour is good to warm up your feet before the difficult ascent. Starting at the **Chata Zverovka cottage** (1,037 m) and walking on asphalt road you will comfortably get to the Ťatliakovo jazero lake (1,370 m) where Ťatliakova chata used to stand. Continue up the Smutná dolina valley on a blue and green-marked trail. Past the crossroads in the middle of the valley and continue following the blue-mark. After a steep ascent at the end of the valley and reaching the **Smutné sedlo saddle** (1,965 m) you will find yourself on top of the main ridge of the Roháče Mts. and you will keep to it until you climb to the Baníkovské sedlo saddle in the west. The red-marked route of ascent will take you from the saddle to the first of the **Tri kopy Mts.** (Three Hills) at an elevation of 2,154 m. The second peak of the three mountains will have to be climbed using the fixed chains. The third mountain is accessible by a footpath, which in places avoids the rocks jutting out of the ridge. The passage from the last top of the Tri kopy Mts. to the neighbouring, and only a little taller **Hrubá kopa Mt.** (2,166 m) is less demanding. Much more difficult is the exposed ascent from a trough below the Baníkovská ihla Mt. to the summit of **Baníkov Mt.** (2,178 m). There are two options to choose from for the return trip. Green-marked trail heads to the south and to the Jalovecké sedlo saddle. If you prefer the basic route, go down the steeply descending footpath to the **Baníkovské sedlo saddle**

(2,045 m). Yellow-marked path will bring you back to the Roháčska dolina valley from the main ridge. While descending down the **Spálená dolina valley** you will have two opportunities to use the time to visit the Roháčské plesá lakes before the dusk. But it is more probable that because of fatigue and an advanced afternoon hour you will rather keep to the basic route and return passing by the **Roháčsky vodopád waterfall** to Adamcuľa (1,180 m). From there you will comfortably reach the aim next to the **Chata Zverovka cottage** (1,037 m) even in dark.

Roháčsky vodopád waterfall

27 The Roháčske plesá lakes

Chata Zverovka – Adamcuľa – Spálená dolina – Roháčske plesá – Ťatliakovo jazero – Chata Zverovka

Situation: The Západné Tatry Mts. – North (eastern part).
Starting and finishing point: Chata Zverovka, bus stop, parking lot.
Time schedule: Chata Zverovka – Adamcuľa 1 h – Spálená dolina 1 h – Roháčske plesá 1 h – Smutná dolina ½ h – Ťatliakovo jazero ¾ h – Chata Zverovka 1 ½ h.
Total: 5 ¾ hours.
Elevation gain: 682 m.
Map: Západné Tatry – Roháče 1 : 50 000 (sheet 112), VKÚ, š. p., Harmanec.

Classification: Medium difficult tour with beautiful sceneries.
Basic tour: The route starts at the road post near the **Chata Zverovka cottage** (1,037 m). Start walking on asphalt road in the direction of the Roháčska dolina valley and follow the red-marked route. Ascend the valley passing by the refreshment stall and parking lot over the rampart and in about an hour you will reach the **Na Adamculi crossroads** (1,190 m). Turn right there onto the blue (2764) and yellow (8567) marked route in the direction of the **Spálená**

dolina valley. Cross the footbridge over the Roháčsky potok brook to the abandoned parking lot and continue on the road leading to the forest. Now you walk on a maintained path over the little footbridges to about 18 m tall Roháčsky vodopád waterfall. A detour crossing the footbridge over the brook leads to it. The route continues through the broken forest to the crossroads. Turn left following the blue mark leading through dwarf pine forest and ascend the winding path along the Zelené pliesko lake to the **Štvrté (Horné) Roháčske pleso lake** (1,719 m). Its area is 1.45 hectares and it is 8 m deep. The ascent is parallel to the green mark (5610) leading from the Baníkovské sedlo saddle. The blue mark ends next to the lake and you will continue on the green mark while descending to the **Tretie Roháčske pleso lake** (at 1,653 m, its area is 0.61 ha) lying about 66 m lower and the **Druhé Roháčske pleso lake** (1,650 m, 0,28 ha), which is close to it. Further descent by switchbacks and over a threshold to the **Prvé Roháčske pleso lake** (1,562 m, 2.22 ha) follows. At the northern edge of the lake is the log hut of the Mountain Rescue Service Západné Tatry – north. Descend from the glacier amphitheatre below the Kaktusová hora Mt. to the **Smutná dolina valley** where the blue-marked path (2707) coming from the Smutné sedlo saddle joins your trail. Continue descending on blue and green-marked path in dwarf pine forest on the right side of the Volovec and Rákoň Mts. and soon after you will reach the **Ťatliakovo jazero lake** (1,370 m, area 0.28 ha). Go to the parking lot where asphalt road starts. Comfortable walk on red-marked road down the Roháčska dolina valley will carry you in about thirty minutes to Adamcuľa and you will reach the starting and finishing point of the trip, the **Chata Zverovka cottage** in an hour. Those who are not accommodated at the cottage of Zverovka or in its immediate environs will continue on the red-marked road across the meadow of Brestová, with the Museum of the Orava Village.

Smutná dolina valley

28 The Brestová Mt.

Chata Zverovka – Spálený žľab – Predný Salatín – Brestová and back

Situation: The Západné Tatry Mts. – North (western part).
Starting and finishing point: Chata Zverovka, bus stop, parking lot.
Time schedule: Chata Zverovka – end of Spálený žľab ½ h – Predný Salatín 1 ½ h –

Brestová 1 h – Chata Zverovka 2 ½ h.
Total: 5 ½ hours.
Elevation gain: 866 m.
Map: Západné Tatry – Roháče 1 : 50 000 (sheet 112), VKÚ, š. p., Harmanec.

Classification: Moderately difficult tour, ascent in steep terrain with considerable altitude difference, which is fairly demanding.
Basic route: The route starts at the road post near the **Chata Zverovka cottage** (1,037 m) heading south-westward on maintained footpath following the blue mark (2766) along the fence, across a meadow to the forest below the cottage. Continue in the forest until you reach asphalt road leading to the monument of the Slovak National Uprising (three carved wooden pillars). Yellow mark (8574) turns right towards the Partisan hospital. But you follow the blue mark, which turns left beyond the bridge on a paved road and runs on the right side of the brook below the steep forested slopes of the Predná Spálená Mt. as far as the end of the **Spálený žľab trough.** The road leads in a thin wood to the ski lifts and later across the meadow. Then it ascends to a larger meadow on a little crest. When you spot the ski lift you are at the end of the Spálený žľab trough (1,100 m). Turn right to the trough. Advance on its right side closely above its bottom. Approximately in the half way up the trough cross the draining channel and ascend directly upward. After about a quarter of an hour turn right to a hardly discernible trough. Now you leave behind the forest and continue on steep winding path up the meadows and dwarf pine growth to a shallow saddle on the crest of the **Predný Salatín Mt.** (1,624) with surprisingly fine views of the region of Orava, Osobitá Mt. and the peaks of the Západné Tatry Mts. Continue to the left on the rocky crest as far as the saddle in the main ridge. Turn to the north-west and along with the red-marked ridge trail (0862) continue to the grassy top

Roháče Mts.

of the **Brestová Mt.** (1,903 Mt.) The return trip on the same route as far as the Zverovka alpine meadows takes about two and half hours. You can overnight in the **Chata Zverovka cottage** or in the Primula and Osobitá hotels.

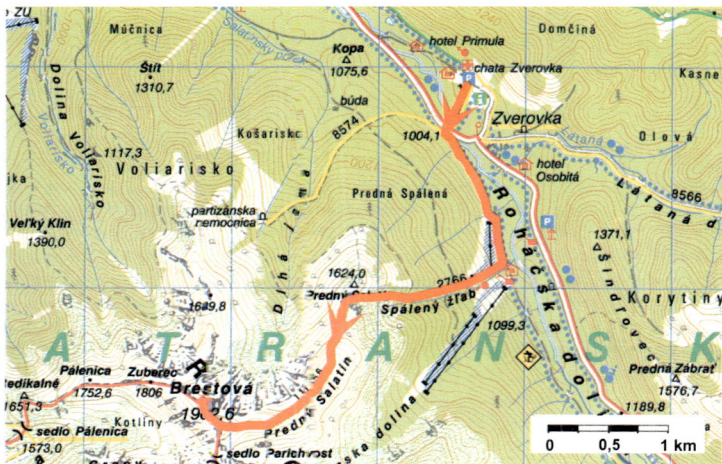

29 Going to the Partisan Hospital

Chata Zverovka – Partisan Hospital and back

Situation: The Západné Tatry Mts. – North (western part).
Starting and finishing point: Chata Zverovka, bus stop, parking lot.
Time schedule: Chata Zverovka – Parti-san Hospital 1 h – Chata Zverovka 1 h.
Total: 2 hours.
Elevation gain: 243 m.
Map: Západné Tatry – Roháče 1 : 50 000 (sheet 112), VKÚ, š. p., Harmanec.

Classification: Easy and little demanding walk in spruce forest with inter-esting views.
Basic route: Start at the road post near the **Chata Zverovka cottage** (1,037 m) heading south-westward on maintained footpath along the fence, across a meadow towards the forest below the cottage. Continue in the forest as far as the asphalt road, cross the bridge and continue to the monument of the Slovak National Uprising (three carved wooden pillars). The blue mark (2766) turns left to the ski lift. Continue on the yellow-marked path (8574) to the right and enter a tall forest The maintained path leads traversing the forest and in places it offers interesting views of Osobitá (1,687 m) in the north and the massive Predný Salatín (1,903 m) in the south. The path will carry you to a hardly discernible grown over trough with a little torrent. Cross it and traverse the forest to the next trough, which is narrower and

steeper. Ascend first up its rocky bottom and then turn right. Continue on the footpath in steeper traverse and you will be coming to the log building of the **Partisan Hospital**. The place is also known as the Dlhá jama valley below the Brestová Mt. This log building served in winter 1944 as field hospital when the German troops attacked the partisan units in the Roháče Mts. It is difficult to imagine that on the premise numerous wounded partisans were treated. After seeing the place return in the same way to the **Chata Zverovka cottage**. The hikers who find the trip too short can also visit the **Museum of the Orava Village** on the meadow called Brestová. It is situated amidst wonderful mountain scenery and the walk on asphalt road (marked in red) leading to it takes about three quarters of an hour.

Museum of the Orava Village

30 The Crest of the Skorušinské vrchy Mts.

Habovka – Javorková – Skorušina – Oravice

Situation: Skorušinské vrchy Mts.
Starting point: Habovka, bus stop, parking lot.
Finishing point: Oravice, bus stop, parking lot.
Time schedule: Habovka – Biedna ¾ h

– Javorková ½ h – Skorušina 1 ¼ h – Oravice 1 ¼ h.
Total: 3 ¾ hours.
Elevation gain: 589 m.
Map: Západné Tatry – Roháče 1 : 50 000 (sheet 112), VKÚ, š. p., Harmanec.

Grade: Little demanding crest tour. The middle stretch of the route between the initial ascent and final descent is very comfortable with little dissected profile. Easy to find your way except for bad weather accompanied with low visibility.

Basic route: The trip starts in the typical village of the upper Orava, **Habovka** (725 m) at the crossroads going to the north. The blue-marked path will guide you up a steep and short valley, which intersects the red-marked trail in the **Biedna saddle** (940 m). Turn right there. Beyond the saddle the crest ascends to the **Javorková Mt.** (1,140 m) The flat top allows only a limited view of the Roháče Mts. From the meadows behind Javorková, however, also the other side is visible where the massive Babia hora Mt. dominates the horizon. After a long ascent you come to the top of the **Skorušina Mt.** (1,314

Swimming pool of Oravice

m) hidden amidst tall spruce trees. The grassy crown of the mountain offers a good view westward. The final stretch initially keeps to the central crest of the Skorušinské vrchy Mts., where the red-marked trail leaves it behind. The descent is mostly on a road traversing the steeper southern flank of the asymmetrical mountain range. The final part of the path brings you to a picturesque landscape with alternating meadows and forests. **Oravice** (790 m) is the ideal conclusion to the outing. Nothing more appropriate than to dip the tired legs into the warm water of the local swimming pool.

31 The Bobrovecká and Juráňova dolina valleys

Oravice – Vanička – Bobrovecké sedlo – Bobrovec – Sedlo Príslop – Umrlá – Oravice

Situation: The Západné Tatry Mts. – North (eastern part).
Starting and finishing point: Oravice, bus stop, parking lot.
Time schedule: Oravice – Vanička ¾ h – Bobrovecké sedlo 2 h – Bobrovec 1 h – Sedlo Príslop ½ h – Umrlá 2 h – Oravice ¾ h.
Total: 7 hours.
Elevation gain: 868 m.
Map: Západné Tatry – Roháče 1 : 50 000 (sheet 112), VKÚ, š. p., Harmanec.

Classification: Medium difficult but demanding tour with great altitude difference and interesting landscape.
Basic route: Start at the road post at **Oravice** (790 m) and beyond the concrete bridge continue on the blue-marked road (2711) southward in the direction of the **Bobrovecká dolina valley**. First ascend in the forest on asphalt road (with no entry for private vehicles) passing by the monument of war victims. Later you will leave the forest behind and pass through the meadow called **Vanička** by gamekeeper's lodge with interesting sight of the Osobitá Mt. Soon you are coming to the crossroads with the yellow trail (8565), which leads to the left to the ending of the Juráňová dolina valley (there is a mineral spring). Its other branch heading to Suchá dolina valley and the Osobitá Mt. is closed for conservation reasons. Beyond the crossroads continue right between the forest nurseries where the green mark (5575) heading to the Umbra saddle turns off. You will continue on the blue-marked paved road on the left side of the brook as far as the crossroads. Turn left at the crossroads, cross the wooden footbridge and the forest road leading alternatively at the bottom of small valley and in the forest gradually ascends. The valley changes into a trough and you are passing through young spruce growth, which later changes into an old forest. The ascent becomes steep and after a while you will have to turn left. A traverse above steep rocks ending close below the ridge follows. Finally the ascent becomes milder and you are walking on a grassy path to the **Bobrovecké sedlo saddle** (1,352 m), from which you can see the impressive and massive Bobrovec Mt. Turn left at the saddle and fol-

Chata Oravice cottage

low the frontier with Poland on the green-yellow marked trail (5575). Now a very steep stretch follows with winding path. Continue in milder rocky terrain. The right side of the ridge is a steep grassy slope, its left side is overgrown by dwarf pine trees. The path passes closely on the right side of the ridge in the upper parts as far as the rocky top of the **Bobrovec Mt.** (1,658 m), the highest point of your trip. The toil was great so are the views of the region of Orava, the Roháče Mts. and the contiguous part of the Polish Tatras. Steep descent to the **saddle of Príslop** (1,382 m) follows. You will leave the frontier behind in the saddle and descend traversing the grassy terrain to the left, to the **Juráňova dolina valley.** Then the steep descent from the ridge of Príslop starts. Coming out of the forest ascend first to a meadow where the path turns right and leads down the valley. Walk first on the right side of the brook to a large meadow, then cross the brook to its left side. Slightly ascending you will get now to the **Umrlá saddle** (980 m). Continue following the red mark (0847), which is part of the instructive hiking path. It will bring you to the lower part of the Juráňova dolina valley, called **Tiesňavy**, which are among the most beautiful gorges in Slovakia. It is in fact a deep canyon cut into limestone rock with washed out "bowls" and waterfalls. The path is in places carved into the rock and you will have to use wooden ladders to pass it. The wooden footbridge at the end of the valley means you are coming to information boards and onto asphalt road. The road will carry you comfortably to **Oravice**, with thermal swimming pool open the whole year round. A bath in warm water will certainly refresh you. You can also overnight in the cottages and car camping site lying nearby.

Gorges in the Juráňova dolina valley

32 The Bobrovec Mt.

Oravice – Tiesňavy – Bobrovec – Sedlo pod Osobitou – Chata Zverovka

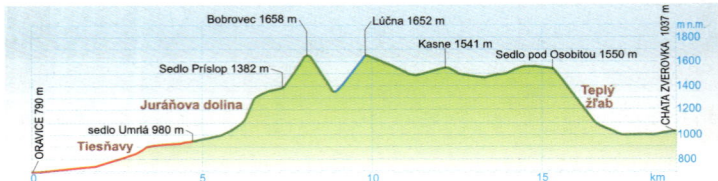

Situation: The Západné Tatry Mts. – North (eastern part).
Starting point: Oravice, bus stop, parking lot.
Finishing point: Chata Zverovka, bus stop, parking lot.
Time schedule: Oravice – crossroad of Juráňova dolina ¾ h – Tiesňavy ¼ h –
Umrlá ¾ h – Sedlo Príslop 2 h – Bobrovec ¾ h – Bobrovecké sedlo ½ h – Lúčna ¾ h – Sedlo pod Osobitou 2 h – Chata Zverovka 1 ¼ h.
Total: 9 hours.
Elevation gain: 868 m.
Map: Západné Tatry - Roháče 1 : 50 000 (sheet 112), VKÚ, š. p., Harmanec.

Grade: Medium difficult, comparatively time consuming with an ascent to the high-mountain environment. It may be difficult for you to find the way in case of bad weather. Medium difficult ascents to Bobrovec and Lúčna.
Basic route: The start is in **Oravice** (760 m) going south-east on asphalt road with red hiking marking which in this area coincides with what is called instructive path. After more than two kilometres turn right. Crossing the footbridge you will get to a wide meadow adorned by groups of trees. If the weather is good you will easily find your way heading to the V-shaped **Juráňova dolina valley** cut in the foreland of the Roháče mountains. You will certainly have no problems to find the entry into the valley hiding in the shade of the edge of the forest. Noise of the falling water announces now something interesting. And indeed after several metres you stand in front of the entrance to an extremely narrow valley between the limestone cliffs. There is so little space at the bottom of the lower part of the valley called **Tiesňavy** that the hiking trail had to be cut into the hard rock. After a kilometre the valley widens and loses its rocky ornamentation. From a shallow **Umrlá saddle** (980 m) on the instructive path separates and goes back to Oravice crossing the Bobrovecká dolina valley. You will also abandon the red-marked trail and proceed by a green-marked one to the **Príslop saddle** (1,382 m) along the upper part of the Juráňová dolina valley. At the saddle you will ascend to the Polish-Slovak state border and follow it over two mountains in front of you. The first of them is the **Bobrovec Mt.** (1,658 m).

It is the introducing mountain of wonderful high-mountain landscape situated above the upper timberline. You will leave the top of the Bobrovec following the green mark to the **Bobrovecké sedlo saddle** (1,653 m). Changing to the blue-marked path you will then ascend to almost equally tall summit called Lúčna (1,653 m) It is a mountain with a rocky summit contradicting its name (lúčna = covered by a meadow). Continue to the north-west by a green-marked trail. The footpath maintains its elevation and does not drop under 1,450 m. On the way you can admire the varied landscape ini-

Juráňova dolina valley

tially covered by dwarf pine scrub, later forest, forest meadows with fine views of the central ridge of the Roháče mountains. Not long ago in the saddle below **Osobitá** (1,550 m) there was also a yellow-marked trail coming from the north over the cliff of Osobitá (1,550 m) which joined the green-marked one. A need of stricter protection of this massive limestone mountain called for a closing of the path for indefinite time. You will certainly respect it and manage to descend down the trough called Teplý žľab. The tour ends at the **Chata Zverovka cottage** (1,037 m).

33 The Kvačianska dolina valley

Kvačany – Kvačianska dolina – Oblazy – Huty – Pod Bielou skalou

Situation: Chočské vrchy Mts.
Starting point: Kvačany, bus stop, parking lot.
Finishing point: Pod Bielou skalou, bus stop, parking lot.
Time schedule: Kvačany – crossroad of Oblazy ¾ h – Oblazy ¼ h – Huty ¼ h – Pod Bielou skalou 1 ¼ h.
Total: 2 ½ hours.
Elevation gain: 210 m.
Map: Chočské vrchy 1 : 50 000 (sheet 111), VKÚ, š. p., Harmanec.

Classification: Easy half-day trip with mild ascents.
Basic route: The route is part of the **instructive path** with several stops. Start at the bus stop in the village of **Kvačany** (610 m) following the red marks (0862) and continue northward to the end of the valley near an old quarry. Then an unusual view of limestone faces of the gorge at the entry of canyons opens in front of you. The rocky forest road gradually ascends on the left side of the brook. You are ascending now and walking slightly to the left in prevailingly beech forest towards the steep rocky bending called Hlad-

Kvačianska dolina valley

106

ká skalka. In the bending of the road you get a nice view of the canyon. But it is dangerous to draw closer to the edge. The easy stretch is followed by another steep bend to the left into a rocky incision. On your left side above the road is a stone **cross** from 1860. This place is called Roháč. This is the place with the nicest views of the canyon at the bottom of the **Kvačianska dolina valley**. Continue on the forest road as far as the turning of the blue-marked path (2708) to **Oblazy** (750 m). Descend on the path down to the brook where you will see the unique buildings of the **log water mills**. After seeing them continue on gravel road along Kvačianka, which will bring you back to the road you have abandoned before. Cross the brook to its left side and after several bends you will see a picturesque valley with a typical village of **Huty** (789 m). After passing by its first houses you will find the turning to the left to Veľké Borové. Continue now on asphalt road between the houses to the crossroads to Malé Borové. The twisting road will carry you to the centre of the village, to the church, municipal office and school. The views of the surrounding slopes with scattered huts are interesting. Then you gradually ascend to the upper edge of the village where the road turning to the right joins other road from Liptovské Matiašovce to Zuberec. Before entering it in the bending turn off to the field road and ascend the crest above the **gamekeeper's lodge below Biela skala** (820 m).

Chočské vrchy Mts. seen from the dam of the Liptovská Mara

34 The Prosiecka and Kvačianska dolina valleys, plus the Prosečné Mt.

Prosiek – Prosiecka dolina – Prosečné — Oblazy – Kvačianska dolina – Kvačany

Situation: Chočské vrchy Mts.

Starting point: Prosiek, bus stop, parking lot.

Finishing point: Kvačany, bus stop, parking lot.

Time schedule: Prosiek – end of Prosiecka dolina ¼ h – Vráta ¼ h – Vidová ¾ h – Svorad ½ h – Prosečné 1 ½ h – Sedlo Ostruhy ¾ h – Borovianka 1 h – Oblazy ¼ h – Kvačany ¾ h. **Total:** 6 hours.

Elevation gain: 772 m.

Map: Chočské vrchy - Liptovská Mara 1 : 50 000 (sheet 111), VKÚ, š.p., Harmanec.

Grade: Moderately demanding tour with not very hard ascent to the Prosečné mountain. The difficult stretches in the lower and upper parts of the Prosiecka dolina valley are equipped with artificial aids. In rainy periods you may have to walk in a riverbed filled with water.

Basic route: An asphalt road will carry you from the centre of the village **Prosiek** (600 m) to a parking lot next to the point where the **Prosiecka dolina valley** (640 m) ends in a basin. It is here where the instructive path Prosiecka and Kvačianska dolina valleys starts and it will accompany you along the initial stretch of the tour and later again in Oblazy. The Prosiecka dolina valley looks like a narrow gorge in which the bed of the brook is squeezed between steep slopes dotted with numerous cliffs. The most tapered place called **Vráta** (The Gate) is wide enough only for the riverbed, which occasionally fills with water and it is also used as a hiking trail. Over the Vráta. the trail sporadically crosses the riverbed via footbridge to the left side of the valley. There is also a rock step in its way, which has to be climbed. Above it the brook occasionally disappears in karst holes and it is the reason why is the riverbed normally dry. At the crossroads **Vidová** is a short little valley called **Červené piesky** with a rock threshold and a 15 metres tall waterfall. After seeing it return to the upper tapering of the gorge. The most exposed part of the gorge called **Sokol** is divided in three rock steps, which are climbed with the help of steel ladders. A fixed chain secures

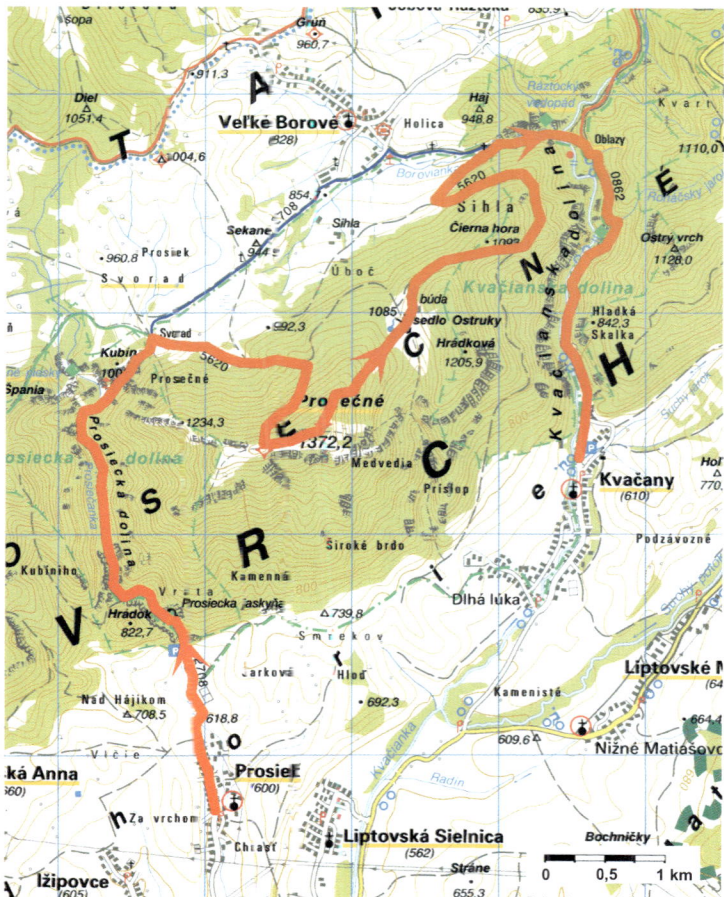

the traverse in one wall. At the head of the gorge the landscape changes. The instructive path leaves the Chočské vrchy mountains in **Svorad** for a while. The basic route continues in the mountain range. It sticks to the green-marked trail leading to the summit of the **Prosečné Mt.** (1,372 m) The route of ascent is not straight. The path changing in places to road is meandering.

The forest around it occasionally opens in meadows and clearings with extremely varied herbs and flowers in blossom. The Jóbova lúka meadow at the summit of the Prosečné, which was a reputed view of the whole Liptov sometime ago is now changing to a forest. The descent from Prosečné is heading to the north-east. The steep path drops to the mountain meadow at the **Ostruhy saddle** (1,085 m), and continues over a terrain edge between Hrádkovo and Čierna hora to the steep forested western slope of the Kvačianska dolina valley. After a short traverse the path makes a loop and returns to the northern flank of the Prosečné mountain and descents in long serpentines to the **Borovianka valley**. Below the village Veľké Borové it joins again the instructive path heading to a couple of log water mills in **Oblazy**

(750 m). After seeing this remarkable technical monuments you have to face a comparatively difficult though short ascent to the steep eastern slope of the **Kvačianska dolina valley** crossed by old stony road from Huty to Kvačany. The road heading to the south enters a beautiful natural setting. The place called Roháč marked with an old stone cross deserves attention as it offers the view of the wildest nooks at the bottom of the Kvačianska dolina valley way down below it. Comfortable road marked in red will bring you to the aim of the trip in **Kvačany** (610 m).

Entry to the Prosiecka dolina valley

35 The Prosiecka dolina valley

Liptovská Anna – Pravnáč – Rovne – Lomno – Svorad – Prosiecka dolina – Prosiek

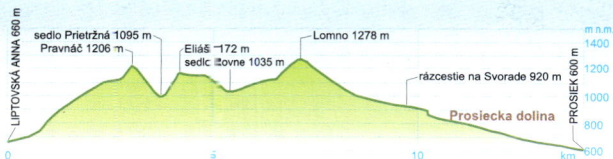

Situation: Chočské vrchy Mts.
Starting point: Liptovská Anna, bus stop, parking lot.
Finishing point: Prosiek, bus stop, parking lot.
Time schedule: Liptovská Anna – Pravnáč 1 ½ h – Rovne ½ h – Lomno ½ h – Svorad 1 h – Vidová ½ h – Prosiek 1 h.
Total: 5 hours. **Elevation gain:** 678 m.
Map: Chočské vrchy - Liptovská Mara 1 : 50 000 (sheet 111), VKÚ, š. p., Harmanec.

Classification: Moderately difficult tour with rather pronounced ascents and stretches secured by artificial climbing aids.
Basic route: Start at the bus stop in the village of **Liptovská Anna** (660 m) and follow the green mark (5320). Walking down the street on the left side of the brook you will get to cemetery with wooden belfry. Continue up the road below the cemetery to its upper edge. Turn right there and go to the edge of the forest. Skirting the forest you will ascend to a little crest. Continue on forest road, which enters the forest. The road traverses above the valley of Liptovská Anna, then it turns left and ascends to a clearing. It changes into a path and enters tall forest and later it becomes steeper running below the limestone walls. Beyond the rock walls the western ridge of the Pravnáč Mt. appears. Turn abruptly to the right under the descending ridge and ascend to forested ridge, which leads to the beautiful cliffs of the top of the **Pravnáč Mt.** (1.206 m). The path turns to the north at the top and now you are descending through the forest and above the cliffs falling to the valley towards the saddle of Prietržná (1,095 m). You are walking on a narrow path, which is winding by the tops of the Eliáš and Heliáš Mts. The path lead to the **saddle Rovne** (1,035 m). Leaving the saddle behind ascent the north-western slopes of the Lomno to a small meadow. Turn right and start to ascend to the crest. Continue towards a meadow, traverse young forest and finally turn to the right ascending steeply across young forest to the tall forest below the top ridge. The route now leads through a meadow mountainside to the edge of the top plain. Crossing it you will reach the top plain

of the Lomno (1,278 m) with wonderful views of the environs. The descent leads through spruce forest down to a meadow. Milder descent follows through beech growth on the edge of cliffs in old forest and continues as far as the rib. Carry on downwards on the rib on a well discernible path, and you will get to the edge of the Malatínska meadow. Pass through the forest to the Skalnatá dolinka valley, which ends in the Červené piesky valley. Continue from the valley eastwards on the edge of the growth as far as the crossroads called **Na Svorade.** Turn right at the road post following the blue mark (2708) to **the Prosiecka dolina valley**. Here you join the instructive path with several information boards. At the upper end of the valley you enter the **gorge of Sokol**. Now you are crossing the oblique rocky bottom on its left side secured by artificial climbing aids. Thresholds of the ravine divided into three rock steps are climbed using steel ladders. There existed a bridge over this part of the valley used for haulage in the past. Once you have climbed the thresholds you will arrive at the **crossroads of Vidová,** where the short valley of Červené piesky ends. There is a rock threshold with

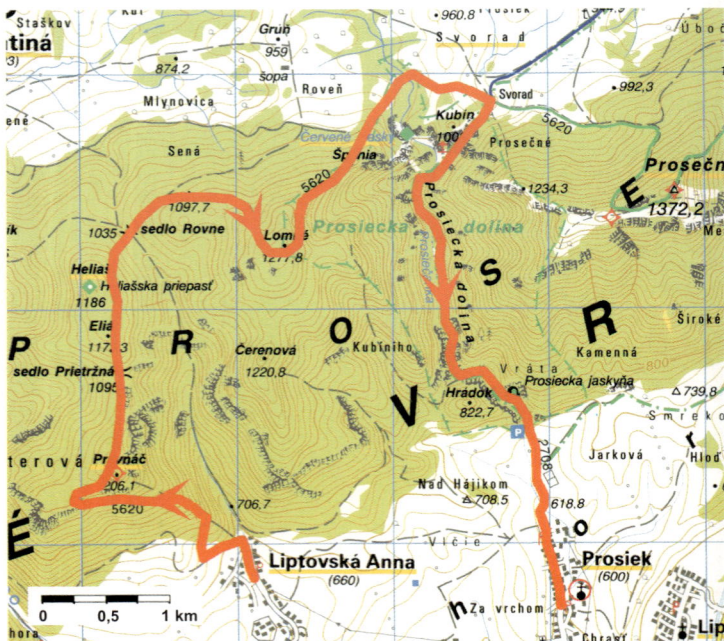

15 m high waterfall. Descend down the valley alternatively on the left and right bank of the Prosečianka brook. Its channel is dry for the greater part of the year and it fills only after abundant rainfalls. Soon you will reach the most tapered point called **Vráta** and on the right side is a somewhat disagreeable traverse and a footbridge, which will carry you to the left side of the Vráta. Vráta consists of two upright rock walls squeezing the brook channel (sometimes with water). Walking on rock steps close to the wall you reach the end of the Prosiecka dolina. Continue on the road to the parking lot and on asphalt road to the bus stop in the village of **Prosiek** (600 m).

Prosiecka dolina valley

36 The Liptovský hrad castle

Kalameny – Poľana – Liptovský hrad – Sedlo pod Kráľovou – Bukovina

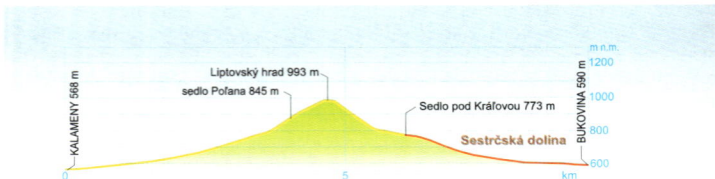

Situation: Chočské vrchy Mts.
Starting point: Kalameny, bus stop, parking lot.
Finishing point: Bukovina, bus stop, parking lot.
Time schedule: Kalameny – crossroads of Kalamenianka ¼ h – Poľana 1 h – Liptovský hrad ½ h – Sedlo pod Kráľovou ½ h – Bukovina ¾ h.
Total: 3 hours.
Elevation gain: 425 m.
Map: Chočské vrchy - Liptovská Mara 1 : 50 000 (sheet 111), VKÚ, š. p., Harmanec.

Classification: Moderately difficult trip with exposed descent from the Liptovský hrad castle.
Basic route: Start at the bus stop of the village of **Kalameny** (568 m) following the yellow marks (8610). Walk up the street along the left side of the church around cemetery and turn left at the next crossroads. Pass above the football ground and below ski lift on a paved road northward to the **crossroads** at the end of the valley of the Kalamenianka brook. On the left side is a thermal swimming pool. On the right side is a wooden cross, the cottage of the hunting cooperative and the right branch of the yellow trail from the Sedlo pod Kráľovou saddle ends here. Continue up the valley and pass by the turns into the side valleys. Beyond the timber stor and a side valley with feeder for game you will reach a distinct bending to the right with a well. Ascend to the right up a fairly waterlogged valley with deep rails walking towards the crossroads with feeder for game. Continue upwards taking its right branch, later turn left from the bottom of the valley on the road leading to the **Sedlo Poľana saddle** (845 m). Passing it turn right and after about 100 m turn left ascending up tall forest between the belts of clearcuts. Turn right under the crest (very poor orientation) onto a hardly discernible winding path. On its left side are steep rock walls so do not go close to edge. At the top enter the conserved remains of the walls of the **Liptovský hrad castle** (993 m). The red mark (0852) coming from Bukovina ends here. The original wooden bridge between the upper and the lower part of the castle is out of use and you have to avoid it walking on the

114

lower edge along the shelter standing there. The lower footbridge over the rock incision is not in good state either. The descent from the castle rock southward over the rock wall is also a problem, you will have to use a piece of rope as an aid. Having climbed down the little wall continue to the saddle and your yellow-marked trail leads parallel to the red mark now. Turn left on the switchbacks through broken forest and passing the crest you will get onto the forest road. The road will pass in a long bend around a log cottage to an open shallow saddle. Leaving the saddle behind continue to the left on forest road down to the road post at the edge of the forest at the **Sedlo pod Kráľovou saddle** (773 m). The yellow mark turns to the west there and continues along the forest edge to the end of the valley of the Kalamenianka brook. However, take the left turn downward and to the east following the red marks and now you are passing through meadows into a continuous canopy. The rocky road continues slightly to the left towards a brook and the following stretch of rough road will lead you to a meadow with timber storage building. Crossing the brook you will continue to the paved road leading to the village of **Bukovina** (590 m).

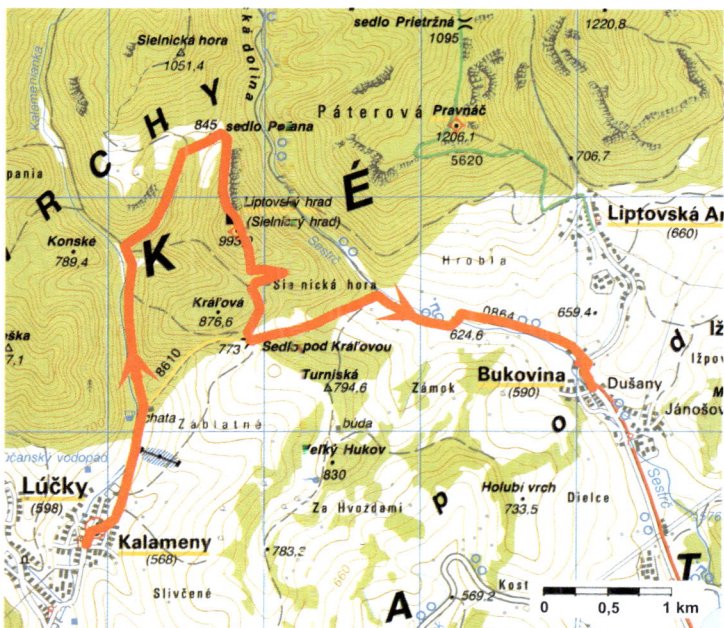

37 The Veľký Choč Mt. from Likavka

Likavka – Veľký Choč – Lúčky

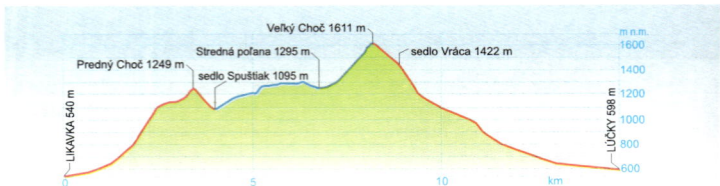

Situation: Chočské vrchy Mts.
Starting point: Likavka, bus stop, parking lot.
Finishing point: Lúčky, bus stop, parking lot.
Time schedule: Likavka ½ h – Likavský hrad ½ h – Predný Choč 1 ¾ h – Stredná Poľana 1 ½ h – Veľký Choč 1 h – Vráca ½ h – Žimerová ½ h – end of Jastrabá ½ h – Lúčky ½ h. **Total:** 7 ¼ hours.
Elevation gain: 1,071 m.
Map: Chočské vrchy - Liptovská Mara 1 : 50 000 (sheet 111), VKÚ, š.p., Harmanec.

Grade: Comparatively demanding tour with toilsome ascent and big elevation difference. High-mountain environment in the area of the summit.
Basic route: At the bus stop of **Likavka** (540 m) choose the red-marked road. The road passes by the ruins of the Likavský hrad castle on its left and moderately ascends in a shallow valley. It steepens only in its head where the steep path traverses a wide clearing and continues in the forest by two meanders. Long traverse follows. It heads to a wide grassy saddle (1,152 m) below the **Predný Choč Mt.** (1,249 m). If you want to get a nice view from the summit of the Predný Choč Mt., you have to make a short detour turning off onto an unmarked path. The red hiking mark joins the red one in the **Spuštiak saddle**. The ascent to the slope of Zadný Choč Mt. leads on a steep unpaved road. When you reach the clearing turn left onto the path heading first to the Zadná Poľana alpine meadow, where the tourist cottage called Hviezdoslavova chata used to stand before the Second World War. Beyond the forest the **Stredná poľana Mt.** alpine meadow (1,250 m) appears and it is the second time you change the colour of marking. Turn right to green-marked trail leading of the northern edge of the alpine meadow. The trail turns left near tall spruce trees and due to the fact that it follows the gradient line the sea level altitude increases rapidly. A sharp right bend will carry you to a traverse. After a short stretch where you have to use also your hands, another traverse follows. Suddenly you realise that you left behind the spruce trees. The dwarf pine scrub all around you announces the summit of the **Veľký Choč Mt.** (1,611 m). If the weather is favourable, you will

Chočské vrchy Mts.

immediately understand why is the place so unique. There are few mountains in Slovakia from which you can get such a panoramic view as from the Veľký Choč mountain. It comprises all surrounding mountain ranges of the Western Carpathians. The Babia hora Mt. and Pilsko Mt. are in the north, in the east you can admire the High Tatras and Roháče Mts., in the south-east it is the mountain range of the Nízke Tatry Mts. The Veľká Fatra Mts. are on the south-west and Malá Fatra Mts. are on the west. Going back you will descend again to the Liptov region, but taking another route. It is the red-marked trail heading to the **Vráca saddle** (1,422 m) in the south with a short rocky crest of **Malý Choč Mt.**

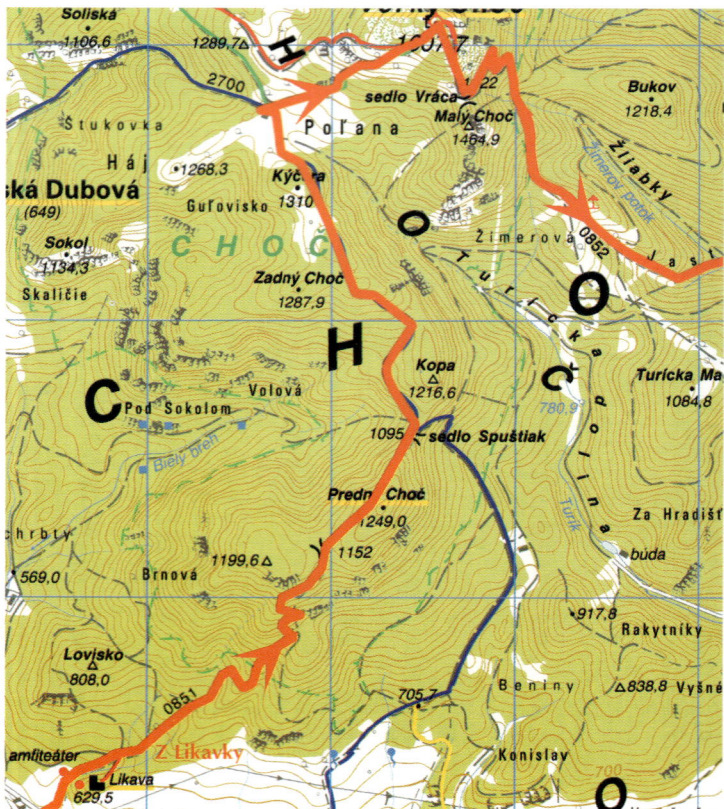

(1,465 m) on the other side The descent from the saddle on a very steep path heading to the east then passes through a spruce forest. Lower ahead the path leaves the steep valley by traversing to the right towards the meadows on **Žimerová Mt.** (1,080 m). The fresh mountain meadows offer fine retrospective views of the Veľký and Malý Choč mountains. The descent continues to the Jastrabá valley, which ends in the bigger Lúčanská dolina valley. There is an old asphalt road in the valley, which will bring you to the spa buildings in the village of **Lúčky** (598 m).

38 The Veľký Choč Mt. from Valaská Dubová

Valaská Dubová – Stredná poľana – Veľký Choč – Vyšný Kubín

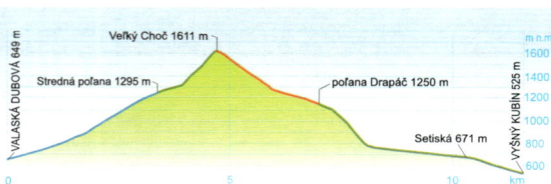

Situation: Chočské vrchy Mts.
Starting point: Valaská Dubová, bus stop, parking lot.
Finishing point: Vyšný Kubín, bus stop, parking lot.
Time schedule: Valaská Dubová – Stredná poľana 1 ½ h – Veľký Choč 1 h – Drapáč ¾ h – Vyšný Kubín 1 ¼ h. **Total:** 4 ½ hours.
Elevation gain: 1,086 m.
Map: Chočské vrchy - Liptovská Mara 1 : 50 000 (sheet 111), VKÚ, š. p., Harmanec.

Classification: Moderately difficult tour with great altitude difference.
Basic route: Start at the bus stop in the village of **Valaská Dubová**. (649 m) on the blue-marked trail (2700) going up the street, crossing two crossroads, continue straight ahead to the valley lying in front of you. Ascend the gravel road running above the valley passing by a hut and protruding rocks. The road tapers and changes into a path and starts to ascend steeply. Pass by the wooden shelter, the spot with interesting view of Valaská Dubová and ascend on a steep path to grassy meadow where there is the border of the Nature Reserve of Choč. Walk on stony path below the top of Soliská (1,107 m) and you will arrive at a short gorge called Tesné skalky. The path is stony and difficult to walk on but after a while you will abandon the bottom of the trough turning right onto a maintained path, which shortly traverses towards the edge of the **Stredná poľana Mt.** (1,250 m). There is a hut, possible shelter in bad weather. Once you reach the road post continue to the left following the green mark (5560), which heads to the northern edge of the meadow. Walking on the edge eastward you will reach a group of trees, turn left and continue ascending almost along the gradient line to a little crest. Turn sharp right and continue beyond the switchback across the broad slope. The trail leads on small meadows and stretches of forest to the steep rock threshold where you ascend using hands to a short traverse ending at the upper line of the canopy. Ascend on a fairly steep path through the grassy mountainside, rich in flora above all in the springtime. Continue ascending through dwarf pine forest and meadows and then there is the last

steep ascent to the top of the **Veľký Choč Mt**. (1,611 m). There are few tops of the peaks in Slovakia matching Veľký Choč in beauty and panoramic views. Having a short rest descend to the road post, advancing to the west on the red-marked trail (0852) through dwarf pine forest and traversing in the southern slope. Climbing down the fissure in the rock use your hands, the trail continues descending and the switchback carries you to a grassy terrace. Pass through meadows boasting wonderful flora and white rocks and enter the forest. The steep grassy crest descends through the forest to the grassy meadow of **Drapáč** and in its middle is a road post. Change the colour of the trail to green (5560). Descend northward into old spruce forest. Continue on switchbacks to a trough and then descending down over the

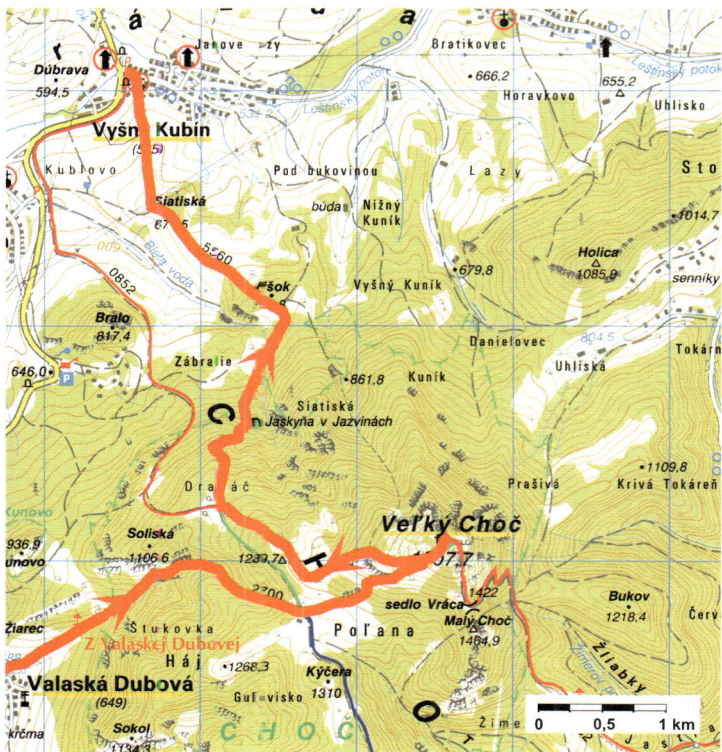

two parts of the Kamenné schody (The Stone Stairs). There is another trough and passing through it you will pass by the Jaskyňa v Jazvinách cave, continue through the forest to the grassy saddle **Pod Vŕšok** (763 m). Pass by its top and walking around the elevation point of Siatiská you will get to the pine forest. Continue on the road leading below the high tension line, along the fence to the church in **Vyšný Kubín** (525 m). Turn right and continue towards the road post. The bus stop is westward on asphalt road connecting Ružomberok and Dolný Kubín.

Veľký Choč Mt.

39 A walk from Osádka to Veľké Borové

Osádka – Malatiná – Veľké Borové

Situation: Chočské vrchy Mts.
Starting point: Osádka, bus stop, parking lot.
Finishing point: Veľké Borové bus stop, parking lot.
Time schedule: Osádka – Malatiná

1 ¼ h – Veľké Borové 2 ¼ h.
Total: 3 ½ hours.
Elevation gain: 381 m.
Map: Chočské vrchy - Liptovská Mara 1 : 50 000 (sheet 111), VKÚ, š. p., Harmanec.

Classification: Easy, half-day tour with low altitude difference.
Basic route: Start at the bus stop in the village of **Osádka** (670 m). You can get to the red-marked trail in two ways. In the first case you start in Osádka westward in the direction of Leštiny and beyond Osádka turn right on asphalt road to Pokryváč. This road will carry you as far as horizon where near the high tension pole on the right you will join the hiking footpath leading eastward on a grassy crest. The other option requires walking eastward from Osádka on asphalt road in the direction of Malatiná. After about 1,5 km your route joins the red mark. Continue ascending right up on forest road through spruce forest and beyond it at the crossroads next to stone cross you will enter again the asphalt road. It will carry you along the Holy Trinity chapel to the first houses of the village of **Malatiná** (803 m). Once you arrive at the road post, turn left onto a field road in an incision and immediately after turn again this time to the right to the meadows and field. Continue above the village. You will arrive at the gas station and start to ascend to the elevation point of Vrchy (927 m). Continue from the Vrchy along the islands of forest first on the left side of the crest then on its right side. Wide meadows offer interesting view of the ridge of the Západné Tatry Mts. and the Chočské vrchy Mts. On one of the meadows (south of the ridge) is a big wooden barn, where a hiker in trouble can overnight. It is popular among film-makers as it is part of the local folklore and its evokes the shepherd atmosphere of the past centuries. However, you will continue up on the wide road through the forest and meadows on the right side of the ridge. The Diel Mt. (1,051 m) remains on your left as you advance across a clearcut. Now you will enter forest and pass through undulated terrain again on a meadow. By passing along its edge you will get to the southernmost tip of the forest. A wide road starts here and you will descend on it through thin growth as far as a tower-like building with wooden balcony (it is a transformation station). You will find yourself near the first houses of Veľké Borové. Continue on the road to a little saddle and turn right next to stone cross heading to the road post. The red mark continues to the left to the village of Malé

Northern slopes of the Chočské vrchy Mts.

Borové. But you will descend down a steep street as far as the typical log houses next to the bus stop in the village of **Veľké Borové** (828 m).

Option: You can continue down the village of Veľké Borové and join the blue

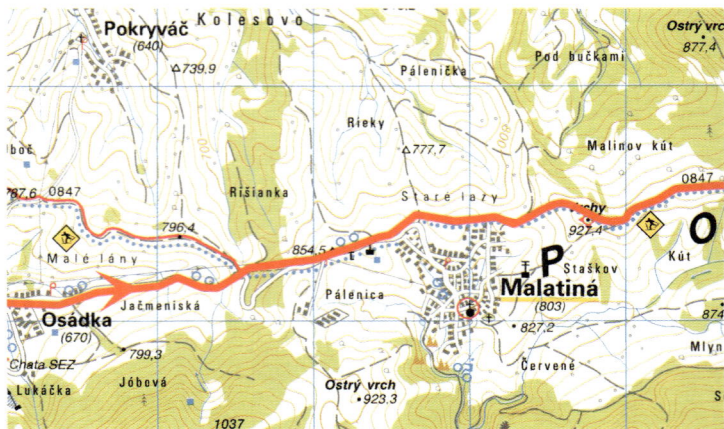

Veľké Borové

mark (2708) at its lower end and descend to Oblazy with historic wooden mills mentioned in the trips No. 33 and 34. Then continue along the Kvačianka brook to Huty or down the Kvačianska dolina valley to Kvačany.

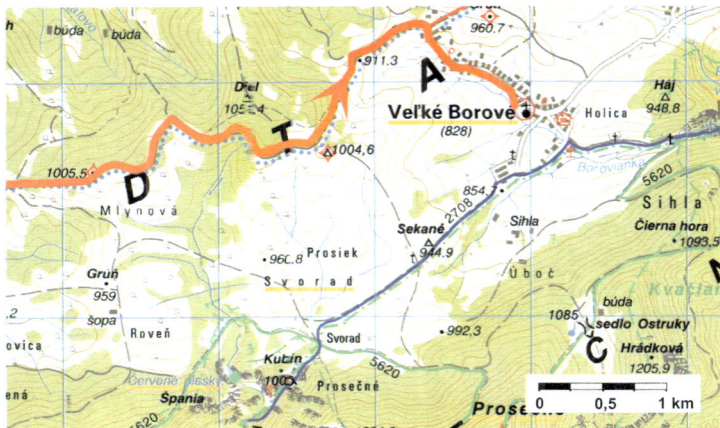

40 A walk from Veľké Borové to Zuberec

Veľké Borové – Malé Borové – Kopec – Prehyba – Zuberec

Situation: Chočské vrchy Mts.
Starting point: Veľké Borové, bus stop, parking lot.
Finishing point: Zuberec, bus stop, parking lot.
Time schedule: Veľké Borové – Malé Borové 1 ½ h – Kopec 1 ½ h – Prehyba ½ h – Zuberec 1 h. **Total:** 4 ½ hours.
Elevation gain: 517 m.
Map: Chočské vrchy - Liptovská Mara 1 : 50 000 (sheet 111), VKÚ, š. p., Harmanec.

Classification: Easy half-day tour with low altitude difference.
Basic route: Start at the bus stop in **Veľké Borové** (896 m). Continue up the street amongst typical log houses to the road post with red mark (0847), which leads up and to the left to Malatiná. But you will take its right branch in the direction of Malé Borové. Take the narrow lane on the right and then ascend to the horizon between the Grúň and Súšava Mts. A wonderful view of the ridge of the Západné Tatry opens in front of you with the dominating Sivý vrch Mt. Babky Mt., Ostrá Mt. and other peaks of the Západné Tatry. You are gradually ascending to the crest passing by the elevation point of Polianky (1,066 m). Moderate descent follows with a view of the basin and a typical village. Soon after you will find yourself at the saddle at the upper end of the village of **Malé Borové**. Continue from the road post on the moderately ascending road. This trail is also suitable for the fans of cross-country skiing. Now you are arriving at the crossroads with a hut. Continue to the right and slowly enter the forest. The forest road is narrow and winding. You are arriving at a small crest below the elevation point of Blato (1,138 m) and continue on the straight forest path. After about an hour walk the red-marked footpath suddenly changes direction. Turn right and start steep ascent, which luckily ends after a while and you reach the highest point of the route the **Kopec Mt.** (1,261 m). This is the point, where also the blue-marked path (2757) coming from Podbiel joins your route. The environs of the Kopec are familiar especially to mushroom-pickers as the surrounding forests and meadows are rich in mushrooms and blackberries in summer. Descend down the forest path and after half an hour you will reach the meadow of **Prieková** in the saddle of Prehyba (1,165 m). Habovka and Zuberec are well visible from this stretch of the trip. Turn off the red-marked path at the saddle onto the blue mark (2689) and in about an hour descend to the centre of the village of **Zuberec** (734 m) over the Črchlica with the view of the ski lifts at Milotin.

Sivý vrch Mt.

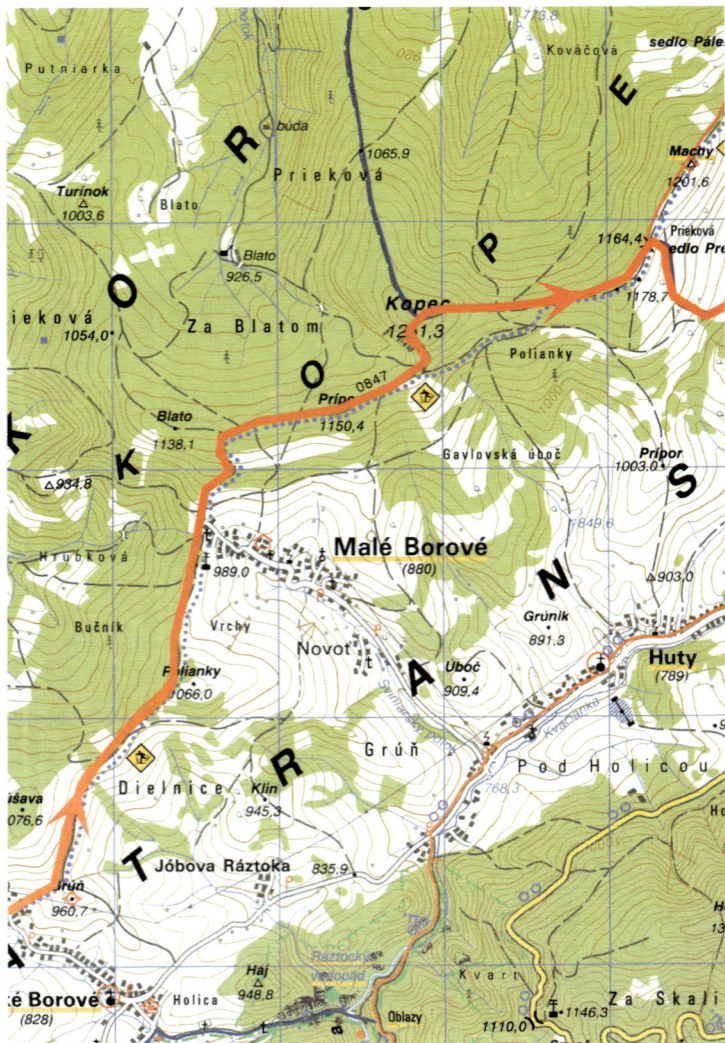

Putniarka

búda

Kováčová

sedlo Pále

1065,9

Prieková

Turinok
△ 1003,6

Blato

Machy
1201,6

Blato
926,5

Kopec

Prieková
sedlo Pre

1164,4

ieková
1054,0

Za Blatom

12 1,3

1178,7

Polianky

0847
Prípo

Blato
1138,1

1150,4

Gavlovská úboč

Prípor
1003,0

△934,8

Hrubková

Malé Borové
(880)

1849,6

△903,0

989,0

Bučník

Vrchy

Grúnik
891,3

Huty
(789)

Polianky
1066,0

Novoť

Úboč
909,4

Kyčarianka

Grúň

Pod Holicou

768,3

išava
076,6

Dielnice

Klin
945,3

rúň
960,7

Jóbova Ráztoka

835,9

Ráztocka
velopád

é Borové
(828)

Holica

Haj
△948,8

Kvart

Za Skali

Oblazy

1110,0

1146,3

13

128

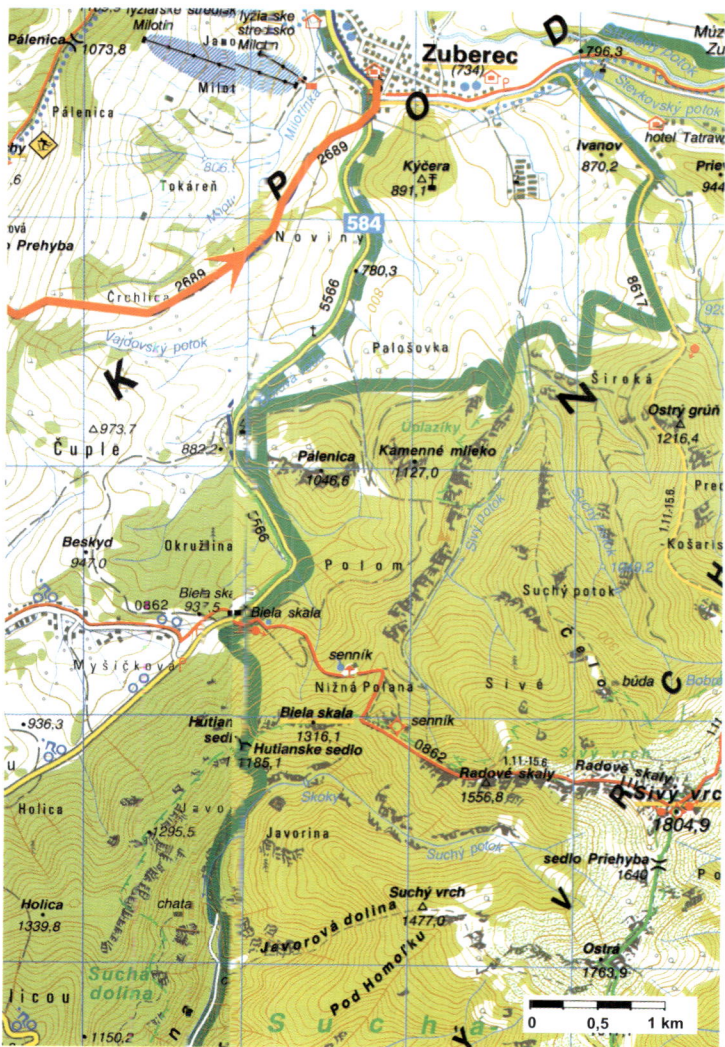

Natural landmarks and points of interests

The West Tatras - South

PODBANSKÉ (950 m, population 50, route No. 1 – 7) is the most westerly located of all the Tatra communities, which lies at the cross-roads of the Cesta Slobody (Road of Freedom) and the torrential river Belá. It is 16 km from Štrbské Pleso and 15 km from Liptovský Hrádok.

Podbanské is frequently used as a base for trips to the valleys of Tichá and Kôprová dolina and to the Bystrá mountain. The **Tichá dolina valley** is today indeed worthy of its name (tichá = silent). It is preferred above all by the tourists searching for a quiet natural environment. In its softer landscape, cloaked by rich meadows, the visitor is more likely to meet a herd of chamois than a group of noisy day trippers. The Tichá dolina valley with its length of 13.8 km and a total area of 52 square kilometres is the largest of its kind in the Tatras. The hiking route traces its whole length from the point where it opens into the Liptovská kotlina basin up to its conclusion below the majestic Svinica mountain (2,301 m) in a boundary mountain ridge. Looking from the Liptovské kopy mountains there are another three lateral valleys ending in the Tichá dolina valley, the highest one being the **Špania dolina valley**. It was given its name by the miners from a community of the same name, near Banská Bystrica, to remind them of their native home. In the bottom of the Špania dolina valley is the longest of the 339 registered avalanche tracks in the territory of the TANAP, which can experience enormous masses of fast moving snow moving dangerously down the valley to a distance up to 3,100 m. Under the big curve of the valley the cross-road board points the tourist to the direction of the **Tomanovská dolina valley** the name of which is related to the miner Toman. A red-marked footpath crossing the valley ends in Tomanovské sedlo saddle a deep, grassy saddle, which with its altitude of 1,686 m above sea level is the second lowest depression of the main Tatra mountain ridge. In the past it was frequently exploited by poachers, and from the path under the saddle the **Tomanovské plesá lakes** can be seen. Two small lakes are the only ones in an extensive system of the Tichá dolina valley. Above the cross-roads under the outlet of the Tomanovská dolina valley to Tichá dolina the valley turns in the direction of the geographic parallel. Both the Tomanovská dolina and the Tichá dolina valleys are closed to the public in the winter season.

The upper section of the massive Tichá dolina valley has an unusual aspect. The bend of the valley ensures that tourists loose their visual con-

Tichá dolina valley

tact with the Liptovská kotlina basin and find themselves as if in the bottom of some volcanic crater, surrounded by high slopes covered by stones, meadows and dwarf pines. The view to the north is particularly interesting, where above the tops of the spruce trees one can see the silhouette of the **Červené vrchy mountains**. This part of the main ridge of the Tatras, between the saddles of Tomanovo and Ľaliové sedlo, is of limestone and got its name (červený = red) because of the typical autumn hue of the grass. The Červené vrchy Mts., along with the Belianske Tatry Mts., are the most important high mountain karst areas in Slovakia with large lapies-fields and deep karst abysses.

These karstificated slopes are not accessible to tourists and there is only one route to the boundary ridge of the Červené vrchy Mts. and then only in summer. Anyone who ascends along the serpentines of the yellow-marked footpath as far as the Suché sedlo saddle (1,955 m) must expect the possibility of leaving behind the calm and silent Tichá dolina valley for the bustle of civilisation in the environs of the Kasprový vrch mountain. Here you will find yourself among the numbers of tourists brought up the mountain by cabin lift from Poland, in both the summer and winter seasons. The end of the valley is called the **Zadná Tichá dolina valley**.

Temnosmrečinská dolina valley

The origin of the name of the **national nature reserve Kôprová dolina valley** is probably connected to the German word for copper, the subject of intense interest to the local miners. The German miners called the valley *Koppertal*. A trip to the Kôprová dolina valley starts at the same point as the one to the Tichá dolina valley. At the cross-roads near the forester's cottage one has to turn to a green-marked path leading along the noisy Kôprovský potok brook. The footpath, without any intense ascent, heads on to another cross-roads and then it continues in a similar comfortable manner. Already the first few kilometres of one of the longest Tatra valleys, will reveal its greatest asset – the distinct natural contrasts of the Západné Tatry mountains with those of the High Tatras. Looking west there is the wonderful view of the Liptovské kopy mountains, while the opposite side of the valley is adorned with substantially more dramatic curves of the cliff massif of Kriváň.

The extraordinary beauty of the waterfall cascades flowing over the high threshold of this strictly protected Kôprová dolina valley can be observed only from a comparably long distance. This is also the case for the **Kmeťov vodopád waterfall** which is a champion among the Tatra waterfalls with its height of 80 m. It bears the name of an important Slovak scientist and a fellow-founder of the Slovak National Museum, Andrej Kmeť (1841-1908). A real high-mountain climb starts only after the turn on to a green-marked footpath ascending to the Temnosmrečianska dolina valley. On the right side of the path is the **Vajanského vodopád waterfall**, one of the most beautiful Tatra waterfalls commemorating the Slovak writer S. H. Vajanský (1847-1916). The **Temnosmrečinská dolina valley** looks like a wonderful natural amphitheatre. Its would-be auditorium is a high cliff with the jutting summit of the Čubrina mountain (2,378 m). Where the stage would be is the flat bottom of the valley and its two large lakes, among the largest in the Slovak part of the High Tatras. The footpath ends near the bigger **lake**, called **Nižné Temnosmrečinské pleso**, with an area of 12 ha and 40 m deep. Another **lake, Vyšné Temnosmrečinské pleso** is situated higher and off the tourist path.

The route to Bystrá starts in Podbanské and goes on following the blue-marked path up the **Kamenistá dolina valley**. This seven kilometre long valley is special for not having any branches. Its slopes remained mostly naked after an extensive fire in 1904. In the upper part of the valley there is a shallow glacier basin and the path ascends from this point to the **Pyšné sedlo saddle** (1,792 m). In this saddle the red-marked mountain ridge track over the Západné Tatry mountains starts or ends the journey, as the case may be. Its route is the most demanding track in the Slovak Carpathians with a total variable elevation of about 2,800 m. The Pyšné sedlo saddle is 24 km from the opposite end of this track – the Hutianske sedlo. The track follows the line of the crest only by a short section from the Pyšné sedlo saddle passing Byšť mountain (2,155 m) to the Bystré sedlo saddle (1,960 m) and goes on by the blue-marked footpath up to the top of the Bystrá mountain. **Bystrá mountain** with an altitude of 2,248 m above sea level is the highest peak of the Západné Tatry Mts. The cone-shaped summit offers a wonderful panoramic view, which in good weather will take in the whole of the Liptov region, a part of Spiš and Podhalie. The shortest return trip to Bystrá is the yellow-marked footpath descending to the small but attractive **Bystrá dolina valley**. In the upper part of the path one can admire a group of four lakes called the Bystré plesá. The largest one of them is the **Vyšné Bystré pleso** lake with an area of 0.86 ha. It is also the deepest lake in the Západné Tatry mountains (12.5 m). At the point where the Bystrá dolina valley opens up into the Liptovská kotlina basin the yellow path crosses with the Tatra main tourist path leading to Podbanské.

PRIBYLINA (765 m, population 1,350) lies ten kilometres south-westward from Podbanské on the road from Liptovský Hrádok near the confluence of the Račkov potôk brook and the river Belá.

The most attractive sight, however, is the **Museum of Liptov Village**, documenting the folk architecture of the Liptov region. The impetus behind the establishing the museum arose out of extensive flooding west of Liptovský Mikuláš caused by the construction of the Liptovská Mara dam, whereupon the main task of the Museum was to save the most valuable monuments of the flooded area.

Tourists know Pribylina mainly as a departing point to the **Račkova** and **Jamnícka dolina valleys** (route No. 8 – 12). A road starting near the museum leads to the Račkova dolina valley. At its end opening up into the Liptovská kotlina basin there is a group of tourist cottages and a caravan camping regularly visited by natives and foreigners. Winter is the time for the fans of cross-country and downhill skiing as there are three ski lifts and well-maintained running tracks in the Račkova dolina valley. At the end of the valley there is an intersection of tourist routes. The red one leads along the borderline of the Tatra National park starting at Žiarska valley up to Podbanské which is not too demanding and affords comfortable walk and offering some lovely views of the Liptovská kotlina basin. The ascent by the green route leading north-west to the top of Mládky mountain and further to Baranec mountain is more tiresome, mainly in the early stages. Tourist prefer the blue-marked path leading deeper into the Račkova dolina valley. The first two kilometres, common for both the Račkova and Jamnícka dolina valleys are called the Úzka dolina valley. It starts at 885 m above sea level and branches to the Račkova and Jamnícka valleys which are 960 m above sea level. In both valleys, separated from each other by the fork of Jakubina traces of glacial activity are evident. From the point where the valley branches a yellow-market footpath leads along the Račkova dolina valley. The first two thirds of the ascent up the valley is comparably easy. The route continues across ever thickening woods to a large, almost flat alpine meadow called Prostredná poľana with an old log hut, testimony that there used to be pastures here in the past. Even further the remains of what was once the highest situated sheep dairy farm in Slovakia (1,600 m) can be found. Past this landmark one can turn to the **Gáborova dolina valley**.

Ascending up the Gáborova dolina valley one can get to the main ridge and further to the Gáborovo sedlo (1,937 m) or the Bystré (1,946 m) saddles. But the most attractive destination for the tourists is the upper part of the Račkova dolina valley via the yellow-marked path. The stony path, crossing the dwarf pine forest is comparably steep making the ascent difficult and straining, but the reward comes in the form of excellent sights of the surrounding peaks of Bystrá, Klin, Jakubina and above all the romantic mountain scenery of **Račkove plesá lakes** at an altitude of 1,717 m above sea level which are set in a distinct glacier kettle. There is a lower situated Dolné Račkovo pleso lake, the area of which is 1.19 ha with a maximum depth 1.5 m. What is interesting about this lake is that during dry spells its water table drops and then a prolonged elevation separating the lake in two emerges in its centre. The Vyšné Račkovo pleso lake is smaller but deeper, reaching a maximum depth of 10 m. A winding path above the lakes leads further to the **Račkovo sedlo saddle** (1,958 m) situated in the main ridge of the Západné Tatry mountains over which the top of **Končistá peak** (1,993 m) towers. From here one can ascend by a stony path (tracing the Slovak-Polish state borderline) to the very top of **Hrubý vrch mountain** (2,137 m) and enjoy the

Šarafiový vodopád waterfall

fine view of the Roháče mountains, the massive body of Bystrá mountain and the furthermost parts of the Račkova and Jamnícka dolina valleys. South of it is Jakubina mountain (2,194 m), the second highest top of Západné Tatry mountains. Ascent to Jakubina is very difficult. It is a high-mountain tour by green mark passing its rocky crest recommended only in good weather. This goes for both, the northern and southern access tracks.

But the most favourite track in this part of Západné Tatry is the ascent along Jamnícka dolina valley following the blue mark. It starts at an approximate altitude 960 m and ends in the conclusion of the valley in the height 1,860 m. Jamnícka dolina valley is 6.5 km long and narrow. It widens in its end under the Ostrý Roháč mountain and Žiarske sedlo saddle, called **Záhrady**. It is actually a kettle and the green mark leading to Žiarske sedlo saddle proceeds along its rim crossing the blue route across Jamnícka dolina valley. This is the most beautiful part of the valley. It is full of variegated high-mountain plants and provides some wonderful sights of Ostrý Roháč, massive Hrubý vrch and Jakubina mountains. The area belongs to the ones with the highest rate of rain in Slovakia (mean annual totals of precipitation is 2,200 mm). The blue mark continues along the Jamnícky potok brook up to the **Jamnícke plesá lakes**. Nižné Jamnícke pleso lake is in the altitude 1,728 m, its area is 1.13 ha and depth is 4 m. Vyšné Jamnícke pleso lake is situated higher, 1,834 m, it is smaller (0.41 ha) and deeper (8 m). Above, along the main ridge of Roháče mountains, a winding footpath leads up to Jamnícke sedlo saddle (1,908 m) which is situated between Ostrý Roháč and Volovec mountains. In upper part of the valley under Žiarske sedlo saddle, in the altitude 1,835 m another little lake is hidden. It is **Žiarske pleso lake**. Its area is 0.11 hectares and depth only 0.8 m.

ŽIAR (765 m, population 420) lies 10 kilometres north-east of Liptovský Mikuláš, not far away from of its namesake valley which opens out into the Liptovská kotlina basin. **SMREČANY** (718 m, population 600) forming prac-

Bobrovecká vápenica

tically a common settlement with Žiar, stretches on both banks of the Smrečianka brook, five kilometres north-east from Liptovský Mikuláš.

Visitors to Smrečany and Žiar usually pass through the communities in pursuit of snow or undertaking walks to higher situated places on the southern slopes of the Západné Tatry mountains. Immediately beyond the community Žiar is a **group of holiday cottages** with two ski lifts and downhill skiing tracks for less demanding skiers. By taking a red-marked path towards Podbanské one gets to two short ski lifts placed two kilometres from the end of the **Žiarska dolina valley** (route No. 13 – 16) at the point where it opens up to the Liptovská kotlina basin. However, the main aim of the tourists and skiers in the area is a seven kilometres long valley bordered in the west by the mountain fork consisting of the Baníkov-Ráztoka-Kečka mountains and in the east by the fork at the Plačlivé-Baranec-Holý vrch mountains. The end of the valley with the Smrečianka brook is at a sea level altitude of 900 m and its highest parts reach an altitude of as much as 1,870 m (Baníkovský kotol). The lower part of the valley is comparably narrow. It widens only in the central positions where there the alpine meadows open to the sunshine. Its ending is formed by a massive amphitheatre with glacier kettles called Veľké and Malé Závraty separated from each other by the rocky crest of the Prostredný grúň mountain. The valley was glaciated up to an altitude of 1,000 m above sea level during the last Glacial period. Its glacial past is well visible, especially in the glacier kettle and near the Šarafiov vodopád waterfall.

A favourite and sought-after resting place in the upper part of the valley is the **tourist cottage of Žiarska chata** (1,300 m). It was built in 1949-1950 on the site of an old cottage of the thirties, burnt down by the Nazis in 1944. Its position amid the mountains represents an excellent departing point for high-mountain tours to the surrounding peaks or passages over the saddles to the neighbouring valleys. It has a ski lift that enhances its attractiveness for winter skiing. North of the cottage and passing the dwarf pines are green and blue marked footpaths which lead up to the bottom of the Prostredný grúň mountain. The ascent is not too demanding and tourists enjoy the lovely silhouette of the surrounding peaks, especially Baranec. The blue track continues further up to the Smutné sedlo saddle (1,965 m) while the green-marked path deviates north-east up to a small wooden shelter about 450 m below the rocky Žiarske sedlo saddle (1,917 m) right below the top of Plačlivý mountain. It is possible to continue along the saddle observing the green mark to the Jamnícka dolina valley or the yellow one over a grassy ridge leading to the top of Smrek mountain (2,072 m). Smrek is usually only a stop on the ridge tour to the top of **Baranec mountain** (2,184 m) also called the Veľký vrch mountain. It is the third highest peak of the Západné Tatry mountains and offers a grandiose vista to all cardinal points. From the point of view of high-mountain flora it is interesting for its diversity, above all in northern and north-eastern parts of the summit, as well as on the south-eastern forks with the most dense growth of dwarf pine preserved in the Západné Tatry mountains. The descent from the top of the Baranec mountain leads along the green-marked track south-eastward to the conclusion of Račková valley. But the descent south-westward is also popular. The path following the yellow mark leads across the dwarf pine forest to the Holý vrch mountain (1,715 m), further on along a rocky ridge and a forest to Stará stávka mountain (1,299 m) ending in the outlet of Žiarska valley.

Another favourite, initially comfortable, but later a bit demanding is the tour from the Žiarska chata cottage to Baníkov which leads along the green-marked path. It passes below the Šarafiov vodopád waterfall, along the serpentines across the dwarf pines up to the grassy Jalovecké sedlo saddle, separating the Žiarska dolina valley from the Parichvost valley. But it is not advisable to continue from the north-western slopes of the saddle to the Parichvost valley as it is better accessible from the Baníkovské sedlo saddle. On the way it is necessary to pass the **rocky mountain Príslop** (2,145 m). Its grassy top provides a lovely view of the Žiarska dolina valley. The final aim for the majority of the tourists is one of the most attractive summits of the Západné Tatry mountains, Baníkov mountain which continues along the rocky ridge of the fork and is very close to the Baníkovské sedlo saddle. Then it is possible to start the descent along the blue-signed route to about three kilometres along the **valley of Parichvost**. This particular valley is a deviation from the Jalovecká dolina valley parallel to the Žiarska dolina valley. Parichvost starts in its upper rocky and comparably steep incline by a trough called Závraty, and progressively descends in a more moderate manner. Nevertheless, the descent and ascent to the valley is demanding, and among the most difficult ones in the Západné Tatry mountains. The impression of the valley is enhanced by the cleft forms of the relief in its upper part and the deep forests in the lower. After two kilometres of descent there is the Hlboká dolina valley deviating to the north with a green-marked route heading for the Salatín mountain. The length of the valley is about 2.5 km and its upper part is at a height of 1,800 m. It is a typical glacier valley and at its end there is an interesting rocky kettle called Vrece (Bag). The name of the valley (hlboká = deep) illustrates its mysteriousness and gloominess ascribed to it in the past by the shepherds. About a kilometre west of the outlet of the **Hlboká dolina valley**, the principal branch of the longest valley of this part of the Západné Tatry mountains is situated – the Jalovecká dolina valley.

The starting point for the Jalovecká valley and the northerly Bobrovecká valleys are the communities of Jalovec and Bobrovec. **BOBROVEC** (640 m, population 1,820) is the largest community and a centre of this part of the Západné Tatry mountain range. It lies in the Liptov basin near the Jalovecký potok brook, only several kilometres north of the city of Liptovský Mikuláš. **JALOVEC** (700 m, population 260) is much smaller in comparison to Bobrovec and lies near the Jalovecký potok brook, two kilometres north of Bobrovec.

In this part of the Západné Tatry mountains the **Jalovecká dolina valley** (route No. 17 – 21) is extraordinarily attractive from the point of view of tourists and visitors. Near its outlet to the Liptovská kotlina basin there is a **holiday area called Bobrovecká vápenica** where besides numerous cottages, there is also a short ski lift available. But nature lovers usually go deeper in the valley bordered by the forks of the Sivý vrch mountain in the west, the massive mountain of Salatín in the north and the mountain fork of Baníkov in the east. There is a yellow-marked path up to the Pálenica saddle on the main ridge of the Západné Tatry mountains. At the entrance to the saddle there are the **national natural reserves of Mních and Sokol** with rock walls and an interesting rocky needle called Kamenná Mara. The cliff walls of Mních and Sokol separate the lower part of the Jalovecká dolina valley from the undulating plain Červenec situated in the west, a prolongation of the grassy peak of **Babky** (1,566 m). The route which passes it is marked in green, starting at the end of the Jalovecká dolina valley, continuing across pleasant alpine meadows and a broad grassy ridge up to the foothills of the Ostrá mountain (1,763 m), the top of which is by-passed by the path on its eastern side and crossing the patches of dwarf pine trees. Later it becomes steeper leading over a stony surface up to the top of the Sivý vrch mountain.

But most tourists going to the main ridge of the Západné Tatry mountains prefer the route leading across the Jalovecká and Bobrovecká dolina valleys. This path continues in a northerly direction along the Jalovecký potok brook up to the steep slopes of **Lysec** (1,830 m). Its massive body represents the south-western fork of the Salatín mountain. It is called so because its summit is bare (lysý = bold). The valley under Lysec divides into two branches: the Bobrovecká dolina and Parichvost valleys. The **Bobro-**

In the Gáborova dolina valley

vecká dolina valley stretches under the Sivý vrch mountain up to Brestová. Its lower part is covered by forests and in its upper part combines dwarf pines and alpine meadows. The glacial activity left here distinctive forms of a modelled surface, as well as two glacier lakes – Bobrovecké plesá. As the lower situated **Čierne Bobrovecké pliesko lake** has water only occasionally it is not quoted among the lakes of the Západné Tatry mountains. The **Biele Bobrovecké pliesko lake**, at an altitude of 1,503 metres above sea level is larger and its parameters are somewhat more significant. It occupies an area of 0.1 ha, its length is 77 m, max. width is 21m and the depth is 1.5 m. The path goes on over the two lakes into a slope covered by dwarf pine trees and after a steep ascent it reaches the Pálenica saddle. From there one can continue north-east or south-west along the main ridge of the Západné Tatry mountains.

The West Tatras - North

ZUBEREC (743 m, population 1,700) is 12 km from Podbiel lying on the main road from Dolný Kubín to the Polish border. It is situated in the furrow of Podtatranská brázda at the foothills of the Západné Tatry mountains, in an area called Roháče.

However, three kilometers from Zuberec, at Brestová, a unique open-air **museum of the Orava village** can be visited. It is located in impressive mountain scenery overlooked by the peaks of the Pálenica, Sivý vrch and Brestová mountains in the

Southern slopes of the Západné Tatry Mts.

south, the Osobitá mountain in the east and the massive Mních mountain in the west. Over an area of about 20 hectares, and on both sides of the Studený potok brook, is a village containing the typical folk buildings of the individual regions of Orava.

Not far from the museum, at the foothills of Madajka mountain in the Studená dolina valley there is an interesting **protected landscape – the cave of Brestovská jaskyňa**. It is the largest cave in the Orava region and also the most important one in the Západné Tatry mountains. Going southeastward across the Studená dolina valley, the longest and most dissected valley of the Roháče mountains, we can see the **protected landscape formation of the rocky Mačie diery** (Cat Holes) on the left hand side, with extremely rare vegetation growing on a limestone basement.

At the upper end of the Studená dolina valley at an altitude of 1,037 m above sea level extends a sunny mountain alpine meadow called **Zverovka** (route No. 23 – 29), the principal centre and natural starting point to all parts of the Roháče mountains. Originally there was only a **gamekeeper's lodge** here and in 1928 a **tourist cottage** was built next to it. In 1944 the Roháče mountains became the centre of north Slovakian and south Polish anti-Nazi resistance, and a group of partisans operated in Zverovka.

At the present time there are numerous options for accommodation in Zverovka available for the tourists, with well accessible high mountain hiking tours. One of them (the yellow marked path) leads across the **Látaná dolina valley**, an eastern prolongation of the the Studená valley. On the left side of the path there is the **nature reserve of Osobitá** bearing the same name as the cliff peak Osobitá (1,687 m) among the the most beautiful mountains of the Orava region. For the sake of protecting the rare flora at the summit, the Osobitá mountain is not accessible to visitors. In the Látaná dolina valley iron ore was extracted in the past and the surrounding slopes were used as pastures in the mid-19th century, but today such activities have stopped in favour of nature conservation. At the end of the Látaná dolina valley, another favourite family walk is to the **national nature reserve of Kotlový žľab**, a trough with original forestation in steep mountain terrain. Tourists who continue higher will get to **Zábrať saddle** (1,656 m) which separates the valleys of Látaná and Roháčska dolina, with the additional possibility to ascend even higher to the easiest accessible mountain of all the Roháče – **Rákoň** (1,876 m). Its peak is situated in the main ridge which forms a part of the Slovak-Polish state border and offers wonderful views of the Roháčska kotlina basin and the Chocholowska valley in Poland. South-east of Zverovka is the long **Roháčska dolina valley** with a paved road leading across it. As far as the scenery is concerned this valley is the most remarkable in the region. There are high quality elevated cross-country skiing tracks, excellent opportunities for walking and an abundance of snow. The glacial origin of the Roháčska dolina valley is obvious for its numerous glacier relief manifestations.

The southern side of the Roháčska dolina valley has several projections which branch out into smaller valleys. The best known are the **Salatínska dolina valley** and the trough of **Spálený žľab**. Parallel to the Salatínska dolina valley are the valleys of **Zadná Spálená dolina** and **Spálená dolina** situated higher in the Roháčska dolina valley. The valley Spálená dolina (alternatively called Zelená dolina or Green Valley, a reference to the deep green colour of its vegetation in spring time) is particularly attractive for tourists because of its bizarre relief and rather wild nature. There are two routes for hiking, a yellow path (leading to the Baníkovské sedlo saddle – 2,045 m) and a blue-marked one (which leads to the Roháčske plesá lakes). The Spálená dolina valley, together with the higher situated **Smutná dolina valley**, in the upper part of the Roháčska dolina valley, and the contiguous peaks, form the **national nature reserve of the Roháčské plesá lakes**. It extends over an area of almost 452 hectares, which from a scenic and a scientific point of view, is one of the most valuable landscapes, not only in the Roháče mountains, but throughout the Západné Tatry mountains. Visitors can familiarise themselves with it by using the **tourist path with information boards,** leading from the conclusion of the Roháčska dolina valley to the Spálená dolina valley, which passes the lower part of the valley Smutná dolina beside the Roháčske plesá lakes and ends in the alpine meadow of Adamcuľa. The tour is not exacting and passes the most interesting and most beautiful parts of the reserve. The instruction boards display the geomorphologic, climatologic, hydrological, botanical, zoologic and historical characteristics of the territory of Roháče mountains. The route begins at the point where the cottage Ťatliakova chata used to stand (it burnt down in 1963) and where the Roháčska dolina valley passes over to the Smutná dolina valley. From here it continues along the Ťatliakovo jazierko lake (1,370 m above sea level, covering an area 0.28 ha, at a depth of 1.2 m, and colloquially called The Black Pond) to the Roháčske plesá lakes, remnants of the Glacial period in the Tatra territory. The **first Roháčske pleso** lake lies at an altitude of 1,562 m above sea level, its area is 2.22 ha, and its depth is 6.5 m. The **second** and the **third** Roháčske pleso lakes are at an altitude of 1,650 m and 1,653 m, above sea level, their areas are 0.28 and 0.61 ha, and are 1.3 m and 3.7 m deep respectively. The **fourth** Roháčske pleso lake is the highest at an altitude of 1,719 m, above sea level with an area of 1.45 ha, and it is 8.1 m deep. All lakes, partially silted by the remains of the moraines are situated in a kettle hollowed by the glacier.

More sturdy tourists usually continue to follow the blue path up the Smutná dolina valley to the **Smutné sedlo saddle** (1,963 m) in the main ridge of the Západné Tatry mountains. The saddle provides the best possible passage between north and south. Excellent skiers like to ski in upper part of the Smutná dolina valley, but they have to carry their equipment on their backs. A tour tracing the ridge is possible in a north-easterly direction to the Volovec mountain or by taking the north-western route to the Baníkov mountain and the Baníkovské sedlo saddle.

The first peak of the main ridge of Roháče mountains, east of Smutné sedlo saddle, is the **Plačlivé mountain** (2,125 m). It is a sharp and cliffy peak which was once also called Plačlivô or Plačlivý Roháč. Together with the **Ostrý Roháč mountain** (2,088 m) they form the typical mountain silhouette of the Roháče mountains and the Západné Tatry mountains. The view from Plačlivé is broader than from Ostrý Roháč and especially the vista over the Smutná dolina valley, which is a captivating experience of beautiful natural scenery. The Ostrý Roháč mountain is a double-top cliff peak, although its crumbling surface makes climbing possible only from the saddles of the Smutné sedlo or the Jamnícke sedlo (1,908 m). For the majority of visitors this is the final destination to the Roháče mountains, even though some sections of the track are rather exposed and secured by chains. But the rare prospect of seeing chamois and mountain marmot make the experience worthwhile. The third mountain of the Roháče triplet is the **Volovec mountain** (2,063 m), a massive mountain which spreads over the Slovak-Polish border. It is, for the most part, a deforested, steep, dome-shaped mountain rendering perhaps the most exquisite view when compared to the rest of peaks in the Západné Tatry mountains, and where one can see the valleys of Roháčska dolina, Jamnícka dolina and Chocholowska dolina. The descent is possible by the Rákoň and Zábrať saddle to the valleys of Roháčska dolina or Látaná dolina continuing on to Zverovka.

Departing from the Smutné sedlo saddle some sturdy tourists can undertake a very exacting tour with several exposed points, secured by chains, to the **Baníkovské sedlo saddle**.

Ťatliakovo jazero lake

The first ascent is to the tripple topped expanded rock formation (Prvá, Druhá and Tretia kopa) called the **Tri kopy mountain** (2,136 m). In the north-east a rocky projection called Zelené separates the kettle of the Roháčske plesá lakes from the Smutná dolina valley. The passage over the ridge from Tri kopy is demanding and not suitable for the casual and ill-equipped hiker. Alternately, the passage to the neighbouring **Hrubá kopa mountain** (2,166 m) is easier and leads mostly through grassy slopes. Somewhat more difficult is the tour to **Baníkov mountain** (2,178 m), the highest peak of this part of the Západné Tatry mountains ascending over awkward scales, which in places are secured by chains.

The best start for the tour to the westernmost part of the Západné Tatry mountains is the gamekeeper's lodge below Biela skala, situated several kilometres south of Zuberec, near the paved road to the city of Liptovský Mikuláš. The red marked path leads from the lodge to the forest, ascending to a steep slope and ending in a grassy saddle under the **Biela skala mountain** (1 316 m, route No. 22). The location offers a wonderful view of the Biela skala cliffs the highest peak of the mountain range. The people living in Zuberec also called it Jánošik's rock after an old legend of the Slovak folk hero – the forest robber Juraj Jánošik who hid his treasure under Biela

Below the ridge of the Západné Tatry Mts.

skala. Its almost two kilometres long ridge astonishes the eye with a variation of bizarre limestone rocks and grassy alpine meadows containing a plethora of protected flora. A well-maintained path leads from Biela skala along a mountain ridge providing a magnificent view over the valleys of the Orava and Váh rivers and practically all of the Orava and Liptov regions. Some parts of the path are more exposed encountering various dolomite towers and fissures. This part of the tour is called "Skalné mesto" (Rocky City) and opens the way to the **Sivý vrch mountain** (1,805 m). The ridge including its forks covering an area of almost 113 hectares nature reserve of Sivý vrch. It is a protected area because of its bizarre formations (cliffs, karst forms, rock sites, etc.) with exceptionally variegated calciphilous high mountain flora.

Advancing along the ridge of the Západné Tatry mountains over the sedlo Pálenica saddle (1,570 m, an old historical route from Orava to Liptov, which is seldom used today) the red-marked path leads to the **Zuberec mountain** (1,806 m) and further to the **Brestová mountain** (1,902 m). From here one can descend from its summit following the blue marked path to Zverovka, or for the more fitter hiker, there is the alternative treck southeast over the **Parichvost saddle** (1,870 m), along the ridge. There is also a more moderately difficult ascent to the top of the **Salatín mountain** (2,048 m) with steep faces on the northern and southern sides, followed by a pass over the **Skrinarky ridge**. This tour is considered the most exposed though also the most beautiful in the Západné Tatry mountains, especially the parts over what is called Zvon (the Bell) – distinct rocky formations hanging over the valley Predná Spálená dolina and around Červená skala which are among the most exposed parts of the main ridge. In the following peak of the **Spálená mountain** (2,083 m) the main ridge bends from the east to the south-west towards the **Pachoľa peak** (2,166 m) which has a regular pyramidal shape and offers a splendid view of the surrounding landscape. The descent is comfortable and ends in the Baníkovské sedlo saddle or further on into the valleys of Orava or Liptov.

HABOVKA (725 m, population 1,200, route No. 30) is situated only one kilometre south-west of Zuberec on the way to Podbiel, eleven kilometres distant. It is situated on the confluence of the Blatná brook and the Studený potok brook beside the Skorušinské vrchy mountains and the Podtatranská brázda furrow.

North-east of Habovka lies the holiday community of **Oravice** (790 m). Its precise location is in the furrow Podtatranská brázda 10 km from Habovka and 6 km south of Vitanová in the valley of the Oravica brook and is a part of the territory of the town of Tvrdošín. The most attractive feature about Oravice is its geo-thermal water spring (the temperature of the water is 54°C and its yield is 120 l/sec). Progressively additional cottages, a swimming pool with thermal water, open all the year round, a ski lift, car-camping, and playgrounds now make of Oravice a favourite holiday and tourist resort.

For lovers of hiking Oravice represents a starting point to the picturesque and secluded corners of the Tichá, Juráňova, Bobrovecká, Suchá and Mihulčia dolina valleys offering wonderful scenery full of multifarious gorges. The yellow-marked footpath from Oravice to the north-east and the state border with Poland, continuing by a field road to the border crossing in Suchá hora, is not a exacting tour. Along the route, especially in May, tourists can admire a lovely view of the snow-capped Tatra mountains contrasting with the green colour of the surrounding meadows. A walk to the **Magura mountain** (1,232 m) located on the Slovak-Polish state border, east from Oravice, is also not exacting.

However, a more demanding tour is from Oravice to the **Juráňova dolina valley** (route No. 32) and the **Bobrovec mountain** (1,666 m). It is marked in red and starts at the Oravice chata cottage, heading to the Tichá dolina valley, bending towards the Šatanová alpine meadow, which continues further southward to the Juráňova dolina valley and ends in the one-kilometre long gorge of **Tiesňavy**. The path here is interrupted by numerous bridges. Tiesňava in the Juráňova dolina valley is a narrow canyon with hollowed basins known among the local people as "giant pots" which have little waterfalls. It is considered to be one of the most beautiful gorges in Slovakia. The path leading over the right slope of the gorge is carved in the rock face and is secured by banisters and in places also by ladders. In the past the gorge was used for transporting wood, by means of rolling it down the slopes, over a kilometre-long wooden bridge, the remains of which still exist. Diverse calciphilous plant communities grow here at an altitude of 900 m, though they are rather typical for much higher locations, and are well worth a mention, which exist here because of the cold micro-climate of the gorge where snow lasts longer and less sunshine enters in summer. Beyond the gorge the Juráňova dolina valley broadens and meadows alternate with forests. The green-marked path leads to the Príslop saddle on the Slovak-Polish state border and continues across a thin forest, alpine meadows, and dwarf pine trees to the top of the Bobrovec mountain. The second path leads below the Hrubý vrch mountain (1,327 m) to the grassy **Bobrovecké sedlo saddle** (1,355 m) from where there is the possibility to continue either to the north-east arriving to Bobrovec or to the south-west ending in Lúčna (1,652 m).

Also the blue-marked route across the **Bobrovecká dolina valley** (route No. 31) leads from Oravice to the Bobrovecké sedlo saddle. Its length is about five kilometres. Again the gorges formed by the rock Skalka and its cliffs are among the most beautiful parts of the valley. In its upper part the valley broadens and the path continues across the forest and clearings to the Bobrovecké sedlo saddle. At the end of the Bobrovecká dolina valley the path divides and turns to the neighbouring **national nature reserve Tichá dolina valley** with a path leading along the rocks called Cigánka and over the grassy trough of Široký žľab up to the top of the Osobitá mountain. The last of the valleys around Oravice is the **valley of Mihulčie** dividing the Západné Tatry mountains from the Skorušinské vrchy mountains. Together with the Blatná dolina valley it connects Oravice with Habovka. Here there is a paved road used mostly by cyclists. There are several cyclist routes in the environs of Oravice, Habovka and Zuberec (for instance in the Roháčska, Tichá dolina valleys, below the Skorušiná mountain) and more and more visitors from the Orava part of the Západné Tatry mountains dedicate themselves to this particular sport. Its wonderful natural setting and numerous quiet corners offer abundant and impressive experiences for the ardent cyclist.

The Chočské vrchy Mts.

This road passed also **BUKOVINA** (590 m, population 510) situated at the foothills of Chočské vrchy mountains.The medieval road continued from Bukovina past Liptov Castle, across the **Sestrčská dolina valley** along a brook of the same name. A walk over the valley rimmed by limestone rocks with relic pine and spruce forests, connected with an ascent to the castle

Sivý vrch Mt.

ruins, is a pleasant and refreshing trip and a perfect escape from the civilised world. Parallel to it only several kilometres to the east between the mountain ridge of Pravnáč (1,206 m) and Lomno (1,278 m), connected by green-marked footpath stretches the **Dolina Liptovskej Anny valley**. The name of the valley derives from the community of **LIPTOVSKÁ ANNA** (660 m, population 100) lying in its southern extreme which opens up into the Liptovská kotlina basin.

The most attractive community for tourists is **PROSIEK** (600 m, population 200). But the community is generally known as a starting point for a trip to one of the most beautiful and most visited Slovak valleys – the **Prosiecka dolina valley** (route No. 34 – 35). This karst valley almost 4 km long is deeply embedded between the massive mountains of Lomno and Prosečné (1,372 m). Through the valley leads a blue-marked **educational path** with several wooden panels bearing details on geologic, geomorphic, and pedologic facts concerning the valley and the local fauna and flora. It starts at the entry to the valley consisting of a rock called Vráta (The Gate) above which the Prosečianka brook springs. In its central part the valley widens to a grassy clearing called Polhora on the sides of which are a group of cliffs called Medveď (the Bear), Sova (the Owl), Ťava (the Camel), Jánošík, etc., waterfalls and caves. At

Prosečné

the beginning of its upper part the valley branches out to a little valley called Červené piesky with an imposing 15 m high waterfall and the canyons of Nižný and Vyšný Sraz, which are the most attractive sections of the valley. Their steepness and wildness will most certainly impress any visitor, who will conclude the ascent, and the experience, by the use of ladders. The Prosiecka dolina valley is a **national nature reserve** with occurrences of several rare and protected plant species.

Beyond the upper end of the valley is a grassy plain called Svorad crossed by a blue-marked path heading to the community of **VEĽKÉ BOROVÉ** (828 m, population 100, route No. 39 – 40). Together with another two communities, **MALÉ BOROVÉ** (850 m, population 250) and **HUTY** (789 m, population 220) this place indeed represents an oasis of peace and silence set in the heart of some wonderful nature. They are situated in a relatively forgotten corner, isolated from traffic and the distant settlements. Veľké Borové and Huty are popular as a tourist base for trips to the **national nature reserve Kvačianska dolina valley** (route No. 33). This canyon-type valley deeply cut into the dolomite and limestone rock between the Čierna hora (1,098 m) and Ostré (1,128 m) mountains runs parallel to the Prosiecka dolina valley. Both create a well-known one-day tourist circuit.

The Kvačianska dolina valley has an **educational path** with numerous stops. There used to exist an old road in the valley leading along the bottom and it served as the only communication for the communities of Veľké Borové and Huty with the rest of the world. The landmark in the upper part of the valley is called **Oblazy** – a unique and ancient **wooden water mill**, and another attractive place is Roháč, a rocky promontory in the lower part of the valley and the highest point on the old road. In 1860 a **stone cross** was built here and the place provides wonderful views of the entire canyon. At the point where the Kvačianska dolina valley opens up to the Liptovská kotlina basin is the community that gave the name to the valley – **KVAČANY** (610 m, population 570).

Visitors of this part of Liptov usually make the point of visiting the spa of **LÚČKY** (598, population 1,700) situated under the impressing massive mountain of Veľký Choč. Tourists will certainly enjoy the occasion to ascend the majestic **Veľký Choč mountain** (1,611 m) – the highest summit of the Chočské vrchy mountains. The ascent is rather demanding, especially its first part is steep and tiresome. It starts in a forested valley steeply passing later into meadows called Žimerová. The aesthetics of the green grassland contrasts here by the steep cliffs of the Veľký and Malý Choč mountains that usually are the aim of the high mountain hiking tour.

Lúčky neighbours with **KALAMENY** (568 m, population 450). It originated in 1264 in the terrritory of Liptovská Teplá. The land was obtained by the squire Kelemen giving the name also to the community. The local people were farmers and shepherds. The history of the community is closely linked to that of the **Liptovský hrad castle** (route No. 36), ruins of which are accessible following a yellow-marked path. Liptovský castle also called Sielnický on Sestrč mountain (1,000 m) belongs to the highest situated castles in the Central Europe.

Going to the south under the slopes of the Choč mountains are the communities of **MALATINÁ** (803 m, population 850), **OSÁDKA** (670 m, population 150) and **LEŠTINY** (586 m, population 220). West of Leštiny, under the Veľký Choč mountain and the cliffs of Ostrá and Tupá skala lies **VYŠNÝ KUBÍN** (525 m, population 500). In Vyšný Kubín begins a tourist path to the highest mountain of the Chočské vrchy mountains – **Veľký Choč** (1,611 m, route No. 37 – 38). The green route continues by first crossing the community by a field road from where there is a magnificent view of the panorama of Ostrá and the Tupá skala rocks, which are protected rock areas. As the road continues across the forest the tour becomes a lot more toilsome ascending to Veľký Choč and passing the spruce forests and mountain meadows. In the alpine meadow called Drapáč the footpath crosses the red-marked route starting in Jasenová. The paths separate from each other for a while and eventually meet at the top of the Veľký Choč mountain. The mountain is covered by forests, prevailingly spruce and in the highest parts the only continuous growth of dwarf pines in the whole mountain range can be seen.

Register (The entries are followed by numbers of routes)

Slovník	Słownik	Wörterbuch	Dictionary
brána	brama	Tor	gate
cesta	droga	Weg, Straße	road
dolina	dolina	Tal	valley
dom	dom	Haus	house
hora	góra	Berg	mountain
horáreň	leśniczówka	Forsthaus	forester´s house
horská služba	Pogotowie górskie	Bergdienst	mountaineering
hostinec	gospoda	Wirtshaus	inn
hrad	zamek	Burg	castle
hranica	granica	Grenze	border
hrebeň	grań	Grat, Kamm	comb
chata	schronisko	Hütte	cottage
jaskyňa	jaskinia	Höhle	cave
jazero	jezioro	See	lake
kaplnka	kaplica	Kapelle	chapel
kaštieľ	dwór, kasztel	Schloß	manorhouse
kláštor	klasztor	Kloster	monastery
kostol	kościół	Kirche	church
kotol	kocioł	Kessel	cauldron
kúpalisko	basen, kąpielisko	Schwimmbad	swimming pool
kúpele	uzdrowisko	Bad, Kurort	spa
lanovka	kolejka linowa	Seilbahn	funicular
les	las	Wald	forest
mesto	miasto	Stadt	town
nábrežie	nabrzeże	Ufer	embankment
námestie	plac, rynek	Platz	square
ostrov	wyspa	Insel	island
pamätník	pomnik	Denkmal	monument
planina	płaskowyż	Ebene, Plateau	plain
pleso	górskie jezioro	Bergsee	mountain lake
potok	potok	Bach	brook
prameň	źródło	Quelle	spring
priepasť	przepaść	Schlucht	chasm
rázcestie	rozwidlenie	Gabelung	crossroads
reťaz	łańcuch	Kette	chain
rieka	rzeka	Fluß	river
roklina	wąwóz	Klamm, Schlucht	ravine
sad	park, sad	Park	orchard
sedlo	przełęcz, siodło	Sattel, Paß	mountain saddle
skanzen	skansen	Freilichtmuseum	open-air museum
stena	ściana	Wand	wall
strom	drzewo	Baum	tree
studňa	studnia	Brunnen	well
svah	stok, zbocze	Hang	slope
štít	szczyt	Spitze	peak
teplý prameň	gorące źródło	Thermalbäder	thermal spring
útulňa	chata	Unterstand	shelter
veža	wieża, turnia	Turm	tower
vrch	szyt, góra	Berg, Gipfel	mountain
vrchovina	wyżyna	Bergland	highlands
železnica	kolej	Bahnlinie	railway

Practical information

Horská služba (Mountain Rescue Service)
– Horská služba Západné Tatry – sever, Zverovka, tel. 043/539 51 01.
– Horská služba Západné Tatry – juh, Žiarska dolina, tel. 044/558 62 18.
– Tatranská horská služba Š. L. TANAP-u, Starý Smokovec, tel.
 052/442 28 20, tel./fax 442 28 55.

Hraničné priechody (The border crossings)
- Oravská Polhora – Korbielow (Jelesnia) – nonstop
- Trstená – Chyžne (nonstop)
- Suchá Hora – Chocholów (nonstop)

Chaty - Cottages
– Chata pod Náružím, Obecný úrad Bobrovec 90, Bobrovec,
 tel. 044/559 69 64 – cottage, tel. 044/559 65 01 – Obecný úrad Bobrovec
– Žiarska chata, Žiarska dolina, tel. 044/559 15 25
– Chata Zverovka, Zverovka 375, Zuberec, tel. 043/539 51 06,
 fax: 043/539 53 27.

Chodníky - Paths (closed from November 1 to June 15)
1. Kôprova dolina valley from Kmeťov vodopád waterfall – blue mark
2. Tichá dolina valley from the hut Tábor – yellow mark
3. Kamenistá dolina valley from the shieling to the Pyšné sedlo saddle –
 blue mark
4. Bystrá dolina valley from the alpine meadow below Kotlová to Bystrá –
 yellow mark
5. Račkova dolina valley from the locality Prostredné to the Račkovo sedlo
 saddle – yellow mark
6. From the end of the Jamnícka dolina valley in the direction of Otrhance
 – green mark and to the Jamnícke sedlo saddle – blue mark
7. From the elevation point of Klinovaté to Baranec – green mark
8. End of the Žiarska dolina valley from the upper timber line in the direction of Baranec – yellow mark
9. Žiarska dolina valley from the Žiarska chata cottage to the Žiarske sedlo
 saddle – green mark, to the Smutné sedlo saddle – blue mark and to the
 Jalovecké sedlo saddle – green mark
10. Jalovecká dolina valley from the crossroads to the Salatín Mt. – green
 mark an to the Baríkovské sedlo saddle – blue mark
11. The main ridge of the Západné Tatry Mts. from the Hutianske sedlo saddle (gamekeeper's lodge below Biela skala) to the Pyšné sedlo saddle –
 red mark
12. Smutná dolina valley from the Ťatliakovo pliesko lake to the Smutné
 sedlo saddle – blue mark and to the sedlo Zábrať saddle – green mark

13. Spálený žľab trough from the end of the ski track to the elevation point of Brestová – blue mark
14. Spálená dolina valley from the crossroads of hiking paths above the waterfall in the direction of the Roháčske plesá lakes – blue mark and to the Baníkovské sedlo saddle – yellow mark
15. Látaná dolina valley from the crossroads of hiking paths to Lúčna – green mark and to the sedlo Zábrať saddle – yellow mark
16. Bobrovecká dolina valley from the crossroads below the Umrlá – blue mark to the Bobrovecké sedlo saddle and to the sedlo Príslop saddle – green mark
17. From the end of the Juráňova dolina valley to the crossroads of hiking paths below the Umrlá – red mark

Informácie (Information)

Information on travel and tourism concerning the region is provided by some bureaux of travel information and promotion in certain areas. Information concerning other regions is provided by the travel agencies.
– **Informačné centrum mesta Liptovský Mikuláš**, Námestie mieru 1, Liptovský Mikuláš, tel. 044/161 86, 552 24 18, fax 044/551 44 48, e-mail: infolm@trynet.sk, www.lmikulas.sk
– **Turisticko-informačná kancelária Zuberec**, Zuberec 289, tel. 043/539 51 97, 532 07 77, 0903 548 080, fax 043/539 51 97, 532 07 78, e-mail: info@zuberec.sk, www.zuberec.sk

Múzeá (Museums)

– **Múzeum oravskej dediny**, Zuberec, tel. 043/539 51 49. Opening hours: July 1 – August 31, Mo-Su, 8-18 h, September 1 – September 30, Mo-Su, 8-17 h, October 1 – May 31, Tu-Su, 8-16 h, June 1 – June 30, Mo-Su, 8-17 h.
– **Múzeum liptovskej dediny**, Pribylina, tel. 044/529 31 63. Opening hours: July 1 – September 15, Mo-Su, 9-18:30 h, September 16 – October 31, Mo-Fr, 9-16 h, November 1 – May 15, Mo-Fr, 9-15 h, May 16 – June 30, Mo-Su, 9-16:30 h.
– **Archeologické múzeum**, Havránok, tel. 044/432 24 69. Opening hours: July 1 – August 31, Tu-Su, 9-18 h.
– **Technické pamiatky Kvačianska dolina**, IC Nadácia Oblazy, tel. 044/559 73 92,

Národný park (National park)

– **Správa TANAP-u**, P. O. Box 21, Tatranská Štrba 75, tel./fax 052/448 42 17.

Termálne kúpalisko (Thermal swimming pool)

– **Termálne kúpalisko Bešeňová**, tel. 044/439 24 29. Opening hours: daily 10-21 h.

INFORMAČNÉ CENTRUM MESTA

Námestie mieru 1, 031 01 LIPTOVSKÝ MIKULÁŠ

Tel. +421(0)44/ 15 186, 552 24 18 Fax +421(0)44/551 44 48

e-mail: infolm@tynet.sk www.lmikulas.sk www.icm.mikulas.sk

Free information: accomodation and board facilities of the Liptov region / services / cultural monuments / countryside attractions / cultural and sports events / visit programmes / institutions, enterprises and companies **Services:** exchange office / accomodation / guide service / translation and interpretation service / the sale of educational-promotion material / fax service / sports activities and organised programme: paragliding, rafting, speleoservice, horse-riding, cycle-tourism with a guide, mountaineering, high-mountain hiking with a mountain guide, ski and snowboarding school, ski-equipment hire service, bicycle hire service, panoramic flights, rafting floating.

Rybolov / Fishing / Angeln / Wędkowanie		Turistický chodník v blízkosti / Hiking path in vicinity / Wanderweg in der Nähe / W pobliżu szlak turystyczny	
Stravovanie / Catering / Verpflegung / Wyżywienie		Lyžiarska dráha v blízkosti / Ski track in vicinity / Skipiste in der Nähe / W pobliżu narciarska trasa zjazdowa	
Kúpalisko / Swimming pool / Swimmingpool / Basen		Sociálne bezbariérové zariadenia / Barrier-free baths / Behindertengerechte soziale Einrichtung / Urządzenia sanitarne dla niepełnosprawnych	
Windsurfing		Minigolf	
Turistika / Hiking / Wandertouristik / Turystyka piesza		Paragliding	
Bežecké lyžovanie / Cross-country ski / Skilanglauf / Narciarstwo biegowe		Cykloturistika / Cyclo-tourism / Radwanderungen / Turystyka rowerowa	
Detské hry / Children games / Kinderspiele / Plac zabaw		Jazda na koni / Horse riding / Reiten / Jazda konna	
Člnkovanie / Boating, rowing / Ruderboote / Łódki, kajaki		Počet izieb / Number of rooms / Anzahl der Zimmer / Liczba pokoi	96
Lyžiarsky vlek / Ski lift / Skilift / Wyciąg narciarski		Stolný tenis / Table tennis / Tischtennis / Tenis stołowy	
Informácie / Information / Informationen / Informacje		Volejbal / Volleyball / Volleyball / Siatkówka	
Sauna, solárium / Sauna, solarium / Sauna, Solarium / Sauna, solarium		Káblová alebo satelitná televízia / Cable or satelite TV / Kabel- oder Satellitenfernseher / Telewizja kablowa lub satelitarna	
Požičovňa športových potrieb / Sport outfit hire service / Sportverleih / Wypożyczalnia sprzętu sportowego		Možnosť pobytu s domácimi zvieratami / Possibility of movement with pets / Haustiere erlaubt / Możliwość pobytu ze zwierzętami domowymi	
Hotelové parkovisko – vo dvore / Hotel parking lot, parking on the premises / Hotelparkplatz – Parken im Hof / Parking hotelowy – parkowanie na podwórzu		Konferenčná miestnosť / Conference hall / Konferenzraum / Sala konferencyjna	
Zmenáreň / Exchange office / Wechselstube / Kantor		Možnosť športových aktivít v okolí, fitnesscentrum / Possibility of sports in environs, fitness centre / Sport- Fitnessaktivitäten in Umgebung möglich / Możliwość zajęć sportowych, fitness	
Bufet / Snack bar / Buffet / Bufet		Počet miest v reštaurácii / Number of chairs in a restaurant / Anzahl der Plätze in der Gaststätte / Liczba miejsc w restauracji	55
Sociálne zariadenia na izbách / Individual baths / Soziale Einrichtung im Zimmer / Urządzenia sanitarne w pokojach		Vzdialenosť od autobusovej zastávky / Distance from the bus stop / Entfernung zur Bushaltestelle / Odległość od przystanku autobusowego	300
Spoločné sociálne zariadenia / Common baths / Gemeinsame Badezimmer / Urządzenia sanitarne wspólne		Kaviareň, bar / Café, Bar / Café, Bar / Kawiarnia, Bar	
Kuchyňa / Kitchen / Küche / Kuchnia		Biliard / Billiards / Billard / Bilard	
Chladnička / Refrigerator / Kühlschrank / Lodówka		Maximálny počet klientov prijímaných ako skupina v reštaurácii / Maximum number of clients accepted as a group in a restaurant / Maximale Anzahl der Gäste als Gruppe im Restaurant / Maksymalna liczba klientów przyjmowanych jako grupa w restauracji	R 50
Tanečná miestnosť / Dancing hall / Tanzsaal / Sala taneczna			
Gril / Grill / Grill / Gril		Maximálny počet klientov prijímaných ako skupina / Maximum number of clients accepted as a group / Maximale Anzahl der Gäste als Gruppe / Maksymalna liczba klientów przyjmowanych jako grupa	55

TIK Zuberec

Tel. +421 (0)43 5395197
+421 (0)43 5320777
+421 (0)903 548080
Fax +421 (0)43 5395359
+421 (0)43 5320778
e-mail: info@zuberec.sk
www.zuberec.sk
www.tatrainfo.sk

Penzión U Michala

Ing. Michal Borsik
027 32 Zuberec 246
Tel./Fax +421 (0)43/ 5395 314
www.michal.sk
e-mail: penzion@michal.sk

* Accommodation in 2-3 bed rooms with bathrooms,
  satellite-TV, radio, coffee maker
* Restaurant in folk style with fire place and bar
* Billiards, table-tennis, fitness centre, sauna and whirlpool bath

The mountain hotel Mních lies in the vicinity of Bobrovec near Liptovský Mikuláš.

horský hotel mních

032 21 Bobrovec
Tel./Fax +421(0)44/ 5596611

Hotel-Camp Borová Sihoť

033 01 Liptovský Hrádok
Tel. +421 (0)44/ 5224 039
Fax +421 (0)44/ 5224 055

The area of the hotel and camping site with cottages is situated in wonderful setting on the bank of the Váh river.

Autocamp Liptovský Trnovec

The car-camping site lies amidst beautiful setting on the shore of the Liptovská Mara dam with accommodation in own tents and caravans or log bungalows.

Autocamp SK- 032 22 LIPTOVSKÝ TRNOVEC
Tel. +421 (0)44 / 559 84 59 Fax +421 (0)44 / 559 84 58

HOREC Horské centrum s. r. o.

Žiarska dolina, 032 05 SMREČANY
Tel. +421(0)44/ 5595 227, +421(0)44/(0)905 715 924

The meadows around the cottage are excellent ski tracks and offer unique views of the Liptov region.

HORSKÁ CHATA OREŠNICA, Chatová osada,
Račkova dolina 301, 032 42 Pribylina, Slovakia

Tel.: +421-844-5293 232, tel./fax: +421-844-5293 738
e-mail: oresnica@bb.telecom.sk, www.stonline.sk/oresnica

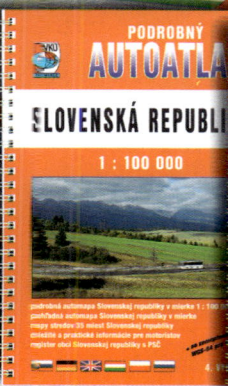

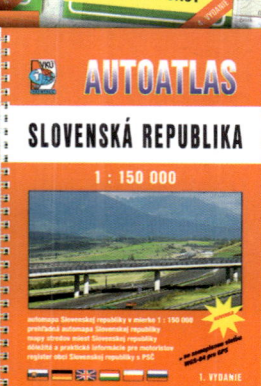

The maps you need

Vojenský kartografický ústav, š. p., 976 03 HARMANEC

SLOVAK REPUBLIC

http://www.vku.sk

distribution   tel.:   00421 - (0)48 - 419 83 38   e-mail: predaj@vku.sk

marketing   tel.:   00421 - (0)48 - 419 83 37   e-mail: marketing@vku.sk

DAJAMA
VYDAVATEĽSTVO

Ľublianská 2
831 02 Bratislava
Tel./Fax 02 / 44 253 182
e-mail: geonad@internet.sk
www.dajama.sk